Convicted Survivors

SUNY series in Women, Crime, and Criminology
Meda Chesney-Lind and Russ Immarigeon, Editors

Convicted Survivors

The Imprisonment of Battered Women Who Kill

Elizabeth Dermody Leonard

State University of New York Press

Published by
State University of New York Press

© 2002 State University of New York Press

For information, address the State University of New York Press,
90 State Street, Suite 700, Albany, New York 12207

Production by Diane Ganeles
Marketing by Anne M. Valentine

Library of Congress Cataloging-in-Publication Data

Leonard, Elizabeth Dermody, 1948–
    Convicted survivors : the imprisonment of battered women who kill / Elizabeth
Dermody Leonard.
        p. cm.—(SUNY series in women, crime, and criminology)
    Includes bibliographical references and index.
    ISBN 0-7914-5327-8 (alk. paper)—ISBN 0-7914-5328-6 (pbk. : alk. paper)
      1. Female offenders—California.   2. Women prisoners—California.
    3. Abused women—California.   4. Sex discrimination in criminal justice
administration—California.   I. Title.   II. Series

    HV6046 .L47 2002
    364.3'74'09794—dc21   2001042820

10 9 8 7 6 5 4 3 2 1

To my husband, Robert J. Leonard, Jr.
for thirty years of love, respect, and support.

Contents

Tables

Foreword

I have worked in the domestic violence field full time since 1981. I have interviewed hundreds of battered women, represented many of them in court, testified as an expert witness, taught Domestic Violence Law at Boalt Hall School of Law (UC Berkeley) since 1988, published the first textbook on this subject (Lemon 1996 and 2001), worked on legislation with the California Alliance Against Domestic Violence, helped edit a national newsletter *(Domestic Violence Report)*, written judicial and other curricula, given dozens of trainings, attended numerous conferences, taught counseling classes for domestic violence workers, and read untold numbers of articles , books, and cases on the subject of domestic violence. Although often frustrating, this field is continually challenging and fascinating, but, overall, it is the clearest example of an effective movement for widespread social change that exists today.

I first heard about Elizabeth Leonard and her work through a prisoner at California Institution for Women in Frontera. This prisoner, whom I have never met, started corresponding with me many years ago because she had heard of my work and we quickly became pen pals. One day early in 1998 she sent me a note telling me about an acquaintance of hers named Elizabeth Leonard, a criminologist who was doing research with battered women at the prison. From the prisoner's description, I got the impression that she saw Dr. Leonard as a friend of hers. This further intrigued me. I asked how I could contact Dr. Leonard and my pen pal sent me her address.

I then had the pleasure of starting a correspondence with Elizabeth Leonard and reading her dissertation, which was a fascinating and important study of forty-two battered women serving time for killing their abusers. As far as I know, it was the largest study to date on this topic. Even though I had been working in the domestic violence field for many years, I learned a great deal from reading the dissertation and I immediately urged Dr. Leonard to publish this significant document.

In addition to the valuable content of the dissertation that has become this book, I was struck by the method Dr. Leonard used in her study. It is an excellent example of conducting research in a way that treats human subjects as human beings, giving back to them through the process, and not just using their stories for someone else's ends. Since my B.A. was in Women's Studies, I was very pleased to see a feminist researcher thinking so deeply about how to conduct research in a humane and respectful way, empowering the women she interviewed in the process. I came to understand why my pen pal thought of Dr. Leonard as a friend. I am now pleased to call her my friend too.

In February 1999, I had the good fortune of seeing Dr. Leonard present some of her research at the annual Western Society of Criminology conference in Oakland, California. That day she focused on that part of her research dealing with the forcible administration of psychotropic drugs to jail inmates without medical justification. The conference audience, mostly criminologists, was as struck as I was by the horrors of this forced drugging and urged Dr. Leonard to present her work to the general public, as part of stopping this illegal and barbaric practice.

Last year, when I heard from Dr. Leonard that the State University of New York Press was interested in publishing her dissertation, I enthusiastically wrote to them, urging them to do so, so that this important work could be widely circulated. I am very pleased that this book is being published. As I wrote to the publisher, "What I like most about this manuscript is that it deals with a very important topic that has not been researched or written about very much. Second, it is well written in that it takes both a global approach to the issue (through the background and contextual chapters), and also a specific and personal approach (through the chapters in which the voices are excerpted). I think this is an invaluable resource to policymakers, scholars, and activists, which is why I have encouraged the author to publish it."

This topic of this book is very significant on many levels: in the fight to end domestic violence, in the field of criminology, in assisting legislators and policymakers when they decide whether to build more prisons or instead put major resources into halfway houses, in uncovering the forced used of psychotropic medications in jails and prisons, and in improving the understanding of criminal defense attorneys, prosecutors, and others who handle these cases. In short,

Dr. Leonard's research and recommendations should be very useful to many people struggling with these issues today.

Since first reading the dissertation, I have started to work more on cases in which battered women are facing murder charges or serving long sentences for killing their batterers. I have also become good friends with a formerly battered woman who was convicted of killing her abuser. In all of this, I have found Dr. Leonard's research very helpful and accurate. For example, she states that battered women who kill "often face a punitive criminal justice system that largely failed to respond to their earlier calls for help." She describes how this system first fails to protect them, then "punish[es] them for protecting themselves and their children." This, unfortunately, is descriptive of my friend's situation, most of the cases I have worked on, and a majority of the cases I have heard about.

The legal system is starting to respond more appropriately to the issue of domestic violence. However, we still have a very long way to go in dealing justly with battered women who kill their abusers. The publication of this book is a step toward achieving that goal.

NANCY K.D. LEMON

References

Lemon, N. K. D. 1996. *Domestic violence law: A comprehensive overview of cases and sources*. Bethesda, MD: Austin & Winfield.

———. 2001. *Domestic violence law*. Eagan, MN: West Group.

Acknowledgments

I wish to thank, first of all, the women prisoners whose participation made this research possible. I am indebted to Convicted Women Against Abuse, a prisoner-led support group for battered women that opened their meetings and their hearts to me. The generosity and openness of all these women contributed to my understanding of the issues explored in this book. I appreciate the staff sponsors of CWAA who helped arrange my access to the group, especially Rosie Guevara and Armando Aguirre. CWAA also introduced me to Gail Pincus and Lani Buccelli of the Domestic Abuse Center in Northridge, California, whom I thank for their encouragement and for adding to my knowledge of domestic violence and women prisoners.

I wish to acknowledge the California Department of Corrections for granting approval for this project, with special thanks to Dr. John Berecochea and Judith Angell of Research Branch for their support and input. I am very grateful to Warden Susan E. Poole for allowing my project to be realized at her institution. I appreciate Warden Poole's professional staff, along with inmate clerks, who facilitated the interview process with efficiency and graciousness.

I would like to thank Ellen Barry, Director of Legal Services for Prisoners with Children, and the California Coalition for Battered Women in Prison for their support of this project. Millie Pagelow encouraged this project with her work against family violence, her professional example, and her friendship.

I wish to express my gratitude and indebtedness to my mentor and friend, Dr. Barbara Bloom, who introduced me to research with women prisoners. She provides ongoing support, invaluable guidance, and an example of quality scholarship. I also appreciate Dr. Barbara Owen for the experience and training I received with her research projects conducted in partnership with Dr. Bloom. These gifted women inspire my work.

Michele Adams, doctoral candidate at the Department of Sociology, UC Riverside, donated invaluable hours of assistance with quantitative data. Her contribution to this research greatly aided in constructing the profile of women participants. I offer a special thanks for those who aided in transcribing taped interviews: my sister Lee Dermody Harper, my niece Tonia Collinske, and friends Debby Jimenez and Sondra Robison. I am most grateful to Christin Hilgeman for her help in creating the index.

This study began in the context of doctoral dissertation research at the University of California, Riverside. Thus, I would like to thank and acknowledge my dissertation committee, Dr. Augustine Kposowa, Dr. Scott Coltrane, and Dr. Jane Mercer. In addition, my heartfelt appreciation goes out to the professional staff serving the Department of Sociology, on whose assistance and support I came to rely during my time in Riverside. Vanguard University President Murray Dempster deserves special thanks for his unflagging enthusiasm for my work. I owe my friend and colleague Dr. Sheri Benvenuti a debt of gratitude for her many years of personal and professional encouragement and support.

My gratitude goes to Meda Chesney-Lind and Russ Immarigeon as editors of this series, with special thanks to Russ for his invaluable editorial assistance with this book. Additional thanks are due to Nancy Ellegate and Diane Ganeles at SUNY Press for their efforts in publishing *Convicted Survivors*. Acknowledgment is due to Beacon Press and to Charlotte Sheedy Literary Agency for reprint permission.

Finally, I want to thank my friends and family for their love, support, and prayers throughout this project. I am grateful to my mother, Hazel Dermody, an early role model for my return to college, who enhanced my love of learning and provided endless enthusiasm for all my efforts. As women interviewees shared with me their experiences with abusive men, I grew increasingly grateful for the men in my life: my father, Gerald Dermody, was a kind and generous man who took great delight in his self-reliant wife, his son, and his three daughters; my brother, Michael, is a loving father and fine male role model for his family; and my sons, Robert and Richard, are fine men who respect the women in their lives. Most of all, I want to thank my husband, Robert, who takes great pride in and fully supports my work. His love for me and ardent support for this project helped me maintain a sense of perspective as victims of severe domestic violence shared their lives with me.

Part I

Chapter One

~

Introduction

Violence against women is a pervasive social problem of extraordinary proportions in the United States. For women, home is a place of greater danger than public places—more dangerous than the workplace, more dangerous than the highway, more dangerous than city streets. However much we would like to picture intimate relationships as a refuge from the violence that exists outside the walls of our homes, all too often the couple relationship itself is the foremost source of danger and threat to women. Men assault their former, estranged, or current wives, fiancées, and girlfriends at alarming rates with near impunity. In the United States, women are more likely to be attacked, injured, raped, or killed by a current or former male partner than by all other types of assailants combined (Browne 1992; Maguire and Pastore 1996; Violence Against Women Grants Office [VAWGO] 1997). Three out of four women who are raped and/or physically assaulted are victimized by current or former husbands, cohabiting partners or dates (Tjaden and Thoennes 1998). Male intimates inflict more injuries on women than auto accidents, muggings, and rape combined (Hart 1990a; Jones 1996; McLeer and Anwar 1989; Stark 1990). Women are more likely to be killed by an intimate partner than by a total of all other categories of assailants (Moracco, Runyan, and Butts 1998). The most frequent form of family murder is a husband killing his wife (Pleck 1987) and the most common form of murder-suicide is perpetrated by a male with a history of abusing his female partner whose attempt to withdraw from him triggers his lethal violence (Murzak, Tardiff, and Hirsch 1992). Between 75 percent and 90 percent of all hostage takings are related to domestic violence (Hart 1990a).

The identification of the abuse of wives and girlfriends as a social problem emerged in the 1970s as the women's movement took shape and moved forward. Since then, the issue of violence between

3

intimate partners has been subject to increased scrutiny. Cross-cultural research reveals that the abuse of women by intimate male partners occurs more often than any other type of family violence (Schuler 1996; Levinson 1989) and is the most common form of violence against women (Heise et al. 1994; UNICEF 2000). Research shows that woman battering crosses all socioeconomic strata; it crosses all racial, ethnic, religious, and age groups (Attorney General's Task Force on Family Violence 1984; Collins et al. 1999; Bachman and Saltzman 1995; Pagelow 1984). Due to the private nature of intimate violence, the actual rates of occurrence are unknown. Nevertheless, known rates in the United States suggest that it is pervasive. Minimally, between 1.8 and 4.8 million American women are abused in their homes each year (Diaz 1996; Hofford and Harrell 1993; Tjaden and Thoennes 2000); and Sherman (1992) observes,

> Up to 8 million times each year this nation's police are confronted with a victim who has just been beaten by a spouse or lover. . . . Domestic assault is the single most frequent form of violence that police encounter, more common than all other forms of violence combined. (1)

The 1994 National Crime Victimization Survey (NCVS) estimates that, in more than 90 percent of violent incidents, the victim was female; women experience more than ten times as many violent episodes by an intimate as males (Buzawa and Buzawa 1996). At least 20 percent to 25 percent of adolescent girls have experienced physical or sexual violence from a dating partner, leaving them at high risk for substance abuse, eating disorders, risky sexual behavior, pregnancy, and suicidality (Silverman et al. 2001; James, West, and Deters 2000). The National Violence Against Women Survey estimates that 8 percent of adult American women will be stalked sometime during their lifetimes and they are significantly more likely than their male counterparts to be stalked by spouses or ex-spouses (VAWGO 1997).

Women who experience a violent assault are more likely to require medical care if the attacker was an intimate rather than a stranger, injuries occurring almost twice as frequently when the offender is an intimate than when a stranger (Bachman 1994). Twenty-two percent to 35 percent of all emergency room visits by women are for injuries caused by domestic assault (Sherman 1992). In 1994, women accounted for 39 percent of hospital emergency department visits for violence-related injuries and 84 percent of the individuals treated for injuries inflicted by intimates (Greenfeld et al. 1998). Flitcraft (1995) reports that a woman who comes to a hospital emergency room three times with injuries has an 80 percent chance of being a battered woman, regardless of the severity of injuries. A survey of Denver emergency departments found that more than half of the randomly sampled 648 women who sought treatment had been threatened or injured by a husband or boyfriend at some time in their lives (Abbott, Johnson, Koziol-McLain, and Lowenstein 1995). Because many medically treated victims receive multiple forms of care and treatment for the same violent episode, "the number of medical personnel treating injuries annually is in the millions" (Tjaden and Thoennes 2000). Approximately one out of four women seeking prenatal care are abused by their partners, resulting in fetal injury, miscarriage, hemorrhage, and low birthweight (American Medical Association 1992). According to Campbell (1995), up to 45 percent of battered women are being raped on an ongoing basis by their partners. Approximately one-fourth of all suicide attempts by females are related to domestic violence (Flitcraft 1995); suicidal ideation occurs twenty-three times more often among abused women than nonabused women (Gelles and Strauss 1988).

Despite overwhelming evidence from hospital records, law enforcement reports, court proceedings, and victim surveys substantiating that violence between intimate partners is primarily and essentially the violence of men against women, a major debate peculiar to America (Dobash and Dobash 1992) concerns the question of "mutual combat" and the related claim that women are as violent as men in intimate relationships (Straus 1993). Men are sometimes physically and psychologically abused by their wives or girlfriends, but compared to most women, they have many more alternatives (e.g., physical and economic) to prevent or escape the violence. Obviously, an enormous disparity exists in the potential of serious bodily harm from being kicked, punched, or raped by a typical unarmed husband or boyfriend versus a typical unarmed wife or girlfriend. Further, in most, though certainly not all, cases of female-to-male violence, her violence is the violence of self-defense (Dobash et al. 1999; Kurz 1993).

Research data showing high rates of female-to-male violence and/or "mutual combat" usually derive their findings from a "gender-neutral" survey instrument widely used in domestic violence research, the Conflict Tactics Scale (CTS). This scale has come under strong criticism by those who challenge the instrument's inherent assumption of gender equality, which ignores the very real physical, social, and power differences between women and men (e.g., see Dobash and Dobash 1988; Ferraro 2001; Pagelow 1985; Stark and Flitcraft 1996). The scale fails to measure intent, injury, or fear, opting to make simple counts of specific acts, such as hits, kicks, or punches, and attempts to hit, kick, or punch. When taken out of context in this manner, a woman's self-defensive reactions are deemed the same as her male partner's brutal and coercive acts. Moreover, claims that women and men are equally violent with intimates fail to consider the prevalence and impact of rape and sexual assault in intimate relationships, virtually all of which are perpetrated by men. Thus, studies using the CTS routinely produce skewed data that promote the erroneous idea of large numbers of violent women and regular mutual combat in battering relationships.

In the landmark work, *The Battered Woman*, Lenore Walker (1979) provides what has come to be the most generally accepted definition of an abused woman:

> A battered woman is a woman who is repeatedly subjected to any forceful physical or psychological behavior by a man in order to coerce her to do something he wants her to do without any concern for her rights. Battered women include wives or women in any form of intimate relationships with men. Furthermore, in order to be classified as a battered woman, the couple must go through the battering cycle at least twice. Any woman may find herself in an abusive relationship once. If it occurs a second time, and she remains in the situation, she is defined as a battered woman. (xv)

Numerous factors influence a woman's decision to remain with an abusive mate despite the likelihood that the violence will increase in frequency and severity over time (Browne 1987; Gillespie 1989; Wilson 1997). In general, the batterer maintains sole control over family finances, restricting his partner's access to funds that could enable her to leave. Due to the nature of the nuclear family and the man's efforts to isolate the woman from outside social support, she has few alternatives to staying in a violent relationship (Archer 1989). Culturally, women tend to invest themselves in their relationships and derive meaning and identity from them. Traditional or religious beliefs, as well as family and friends, often work against a victimized woman's departure from the home and mate. The battered woman is likely to feel responsible for the abuse, aided by the batterer's refusal to take responsibility and by his external focus of blame for the violence. Often the woman believes that her abuser can or will change. She makes every effort to resolve family conflicts and create peace in hopes of avoiding future violence. Abusive events are interspersed among otherwise normal interactions and the emotional attachment the woman feels for her partner can be difficult for her to overcome. She may view her abusive partner as "sick" and dependent on her for survival (Ferraro and Johnson 1983). Generated by the batterer's actual threats of suicide, his threats against her, the children, and/or family and friends, many women remain in abusive relationships out of fear of retaliation (Browne 1987; Sipe and Hall 1996).

A woman with children may be deeply concerned about the well-being of her children if she leaves. She may stay with an abuser out of fear of losing custody of her children, either in the divorce settlement or through later kidnapping by the man; abusive husbands are no less likely to win custody than are fathers with no allegations of violence (Liss and Stahly 1993). According to the U.S. Commission on Civil Rights (1982), "A woman who leaves an abusive situation may be found to have deserted her husband and, therefore, may become the party at fault" (8). While shelters and safe houses provide vital support services for battered women and their children, they have not been able to keep up with the need (Jones 1994); there are about 1,200 shelters for battered women throughout the United States (Crowell and Burgess 1996). Researchers frequently cite the lack of help given to battered women by the police and other criminal justice representatives among the factors that keep women trapped in abusive relationships (Browne 1987; Ewing 1990; Jones 1994).

Many women leave, or try to, only to end up back with the abuser. Women who experience violence at the hands of an intimate partner cannot assume that leaving, by itself, will end the abuse (Foster, Veale, and Fogel 1989; Moracco et al. 1998; Jones 1994). Pagelow (1981) found that almost 80 percent of her sample of 350 women had made at least one previous but unsuccessful attempt to leave the relationship and seventy-one women returned unwillingly. In another study, 20 percent of the women reported that they returned to their batterers at least one time because of threats to hurt or take the children (Liss and Stahly 1993).

Violent assaults may continue after women leave or separate from their abusers. Simply discussing separation or divorce, not only their accomplishment, can provoke an escalation of violence (Browne 1987, Dawson and Gartner 1998; Johann and Osanka 1989). "Separation assault" describes a batterer's violent attack on a woman in order to keep her from leaving, coerce her return, or to retaliate for her leaving (Mahoney 1991). The woman's departure may even further aggravate the man's need to control and to regain what he perceives as a loss of power and possession (Wilson, Johnson, and Daly 1995). Women know to take seriously the threats of their abusive partners; it is possible that as many as 50 percent or more of the women who leave their abusers are stalked (Browne 1987, Walker 1992). Nearly eight out of ten stalking victims are female and most of the offenders are current or former male intimates (VAWGO 1997). Walker (1992) reports that the woman remains at increased risk for at least two years after she terminates the relationship. Further, the National Crime Victimization Survey found that the victimization rate of women separated from their husbands was about three times higher than that of divorced women and about twenty-five times higher than that of married women (Bachman and Saltzman 1995).

Violence between intimate partners sometimes escalates into an act of homicide. Early sociologist Emile Durkheim's (1897/1951) cogent observation, "While family life has a moderating effect upon suicide, it rather stimulates murder" (354), bears witness to the fact that the phenomenon of domestic homicide is not a recent development. Between 1976 and 1996, intimates murdered six out of every 100 male victims and thirty out of every 100 female victims (Greenfeld et al. 1998). According to the U.S. Department of Justice (Zawitz 1994), between 1977 and 1992 the number of male victims fell from 1,185 to 657 and the number of female victims increased from 1,396 to 1,510. In the years from 1976 to 1998, the number of men killed by intimates dropped by 60 percent; currently, women are eight times more likely than men to be killed by an intimate (Rennison and Welchans 2000).

The number of women killed by intimates remained stable between 1976 and 1993, declined 23 percent between 1993 and 1997, then increased again by 8 percent the following year (Rennison and Welchans 2000). The number of white female victims increased 15 percent between 1997 and 1998, making them the only category for whom intimate partner homicide has not shown substantial decline since 1976 (Rennison and Welchans 2000). Estimates of women who have been killed by husbands, boyfriends, or former partners range from 1,000 to 4,000 per year; and percentages of female homicide victims found to have been killed by current or former intimates range from 28 percent to 75 percent (National Clearinghouse for the Defense of Battered Women 1994). However, hard data on women homicide victims or offenders are lacking since, according to Gillespie (1989),

> the primary source of crime statistics, the FBI's annual Uniform Crime Reports, does not break its figures down by sex in all instances and does not report justifiable homicides at all. (202n)

McCorkel (1996) notes the paucity of research on gender and its influence on criminal justice system processes, in contrast to the wealth of literature that investigates the impact of race and class within the system. Official statistics show that the nature of the relationship between victim and offender is unknown in about 30 percent of homicides reported to the police (Laub 1990). In a comparison of the FBI's Supplementary Homicide Report (SHR) with a database of intimate partner homicide cases in Massachusetts, the SHR identified only 71.1 percent of partner victims, and ex-boyfriend cases (one-fifth of partner victim cases) were often miscoded as "unknown relationship" or "acquaintance" (Langford, Isaac, and Kabat 1998). Stark suggests, "there are probably two homicides involving intimates for every one in which a 'spouse' or 'ex-spouse' is officially identified" (1990, 17). Official statistics, therefore, likely represent a substantial undercount of the actual number of intimate partner homicides.

In general, women are less likely to commit homicide than are men. In a survey of nearly ten thousand murder cases, Dawson and Langan (1994) report: women perpetrated 10.5 percent and men 89.5 percent of all homicides. Since 1980, rates of homicide by women have been declining steadily (Greenfeld and Snell 1999). Female offenders tend to act alone and their killings are likely to be unplanned, intersexual, intraracial, with family members and intimate partners the most frequent victims (Greenfeld and Smell 1999; Mann 1992).

Research consistently shows gender differences in the context of spousal homicide. There is a tendency toward more male aggression and more female defensive behavior in descriptions of homicide incidents and in the use of murder weapons. Casenave and Zahn (1992) report that only male offenders commit beating or strangulation homicides; women, on the other hand, are more likely to stab or shoot their victims once. Men tend to be the aggressors in homicide cases even when the ultimate offenders are women; and when males are the offenders, their actions tend to be more violent (Casenave and Zahn 1992). Duncan and Duncan (1978) concur: "Victim-precipitated homicide is significantly associated with mate slayings wherein the husband is the victim. . . . When the husband is the perpetrator, the mate slaying . . . is frequently unusually brutal" (179). Women are at risk of being murdered by their intimate partner when he is suicidal, while male intimates are not at risk when women are suicidal (Block and Christakos 1995; Pagelow 1992). Casenave and Zahn (1992) also found that when women kill, they kill men with whom they cohabit; men kill their female cohabitants, but they also kill their estranged spouses and their girlfriends.

Moreover, women are more likely to kill in self-defense, while men are more likely to kill when the victim tries to leave the relationship. Women who leave their batterers are at substantially greater risk of being killed by the batterer than are those who stay (Block and Christakos 1995; Stout 1991). Wilson et al. (1995) argue that the murder of a woman by her male partner frequently results from his sexual jealousy and/or sense of ownership. Indeed, deadly assaults on a large proportion of female victims concern their attempts to leave the relationship (Block and Christakos 1995; Campbell 1992; Casenave and Zahn 1992; Ewing 1997; Gillespie 1989; Wilson and Daly 1993). Rapaport (1994) reports that, of males on death row for domestic homicide,

> [a]lmost half the men killed in retaliation for a wife or lover leaving them, although the victims of these killers were sometimes the children and of the women as well as, or in place of, the women themselves. (225)

Over the last fifteen years researchers have explored the lives and experiences of battered women who killed their abusive male partners (e.g., Browne 1987; Ewing 1987; Gagne 1998; Gillespie 1989; Johann and Osanka 1989; Jones 1994; Walker 1989). However, research on the lives and experiences of incarcerated battered women who kill has been scant, due in part to their relative inaccessibility. In his book, *Marital Violence: A Study of Interspouse Homicide*, Chimbos (1978) studied thirty-four Canadian inmates convicted of killing their spouses; his study included only four females but all were being beaten or had just been beaten when the homicide occurred. Totman's (1978) *The Murderess: A Psychosocial Study of Criminal Homicide* examined incarcerated female homicide offenders at one institution and found that, of forty-three women convicted of murder or voluntary manslaughter, thirteen had killed a child; thirty had killed male partners, twenty-eight of

whom had been abusive. Foster, Veale, and Fogel (1989) interviewed twelve women imprisoned for killing their male abusers to
determine risk factors for homicide. In sum, only four battered
women participated in Chimbos's (1978) research; Totman (1978)
included twenty-eight battered women in her study, but they were
not the focus of her work; and the findings reported by Foster,
Veale, and Fogel (1989) are limited to responses from twelve subjects. Thus, the current study is the largest and most comprehensive to focus on battered women homicide offenders in prison. It is
unique for its multiple methods, the size of its sample, the depth of
interview material, and for its ability to compare convicted survivors with the general population of California women prisoners.

This investigation begins the process of identifying women who
serve prison sentences in California for the death of their abusive
male partners. This study summarizes data on the phenomenon of
homicide by females against abusive husbands and boyfriends. In-
depth interviews conducted with forty-two female prisoners explore
the link between the women's personal experiences of violence and
its consequences and the social structural responses to their victimization and homicidal self-rescue. The study describes characteristics of imprisoned battered women and is the first to compare them
with the general population of women in prison. This research provides valuable analyses of the experiences and perceptions of incarcerated battered women and describes recurrent themes and
processes that emerge from their narrative accounts. The theoretical
framework for this exploration examines the link between gender
and intimate violence and how this connection works to leave
women without protection while punishing them for protecting
themselves and their children. This original research addresses policy issues that arise out of the analysis of the lives and cases of these
convicted women survivors.

Chapter Two

~

Battered Women Who Kill
and the Criminal Justice System:
A Review of the Literature

Legal Legacy

Throughout much of known human history, traditions and laws relating to marriage have given husbands the right to control their wives, by force if necessary. Napoleon decreed that women must be legal minors their entire lives (Davidson 1977). English jurist and politician Sir Edward Coke (1552–1634) captured the philosophy of male primacy in the home with the still popular phrase, "a man's home is his castle." British common law allowed wife beating but, in a move toward "compassionate" reform, limited the size of the correctional instrument used by husbands to a "rod not thicker than his thumb" (Brown and Hendricks 1998; Dobash and Dobash 1977; U.S. Commission on Civil Rights 1982). The British doctrine of "coverture" determined that a husband and wife were a single legal entity, and that entity was, of course, the husband. Such laws served to codify a married woman's loss of identity and individual autonomy. Under British common law, if a man killed his wife his action was classified as a homicide; if a woman killed her husband her action was classified as an act of treason punishable by burning at the stake (Jones 1994).

American law followed the British legal tradition that supported the husband's right to discipline his wife. It was not until 1871 that an Alabama court revoked the legal right of a husband to beat his wife; in 1874 a North Carolina court followed suit but narrowed the impact of the repeal:

> If no permanent injury has been inflicted, nor malice, cruelty nor dangerous violence shown by the husband, it is better to

draw the curtain, shut out the public gaze, and leave the parties to forget and forgive. (U.S. Commission on Civil Rights 1982, 2)

Until the 1950s, husbands in New Mexico, Texas, and Utah received "special immunity from prosecution if they were to find their wives in an adulterous situation and commit homicide. . . . The same right was not granted to wives" (Dobash and Dobash 1979, 209).

Contemporary Landscape

While American law no longer grants legal permission for a husband to beat his wife, the domestic curtain shows little sign of collapse. According to the 1982 U.S. Commission on Civil Rights, "the laws available for the protection of all people do not protect a woman involved with her assailant in a prior or existing relationship" (2). Ann Jones (1994) observes,

> The constitutional rights of all American women—to freedom from bodily harm, equal protection, due process—and the very lives of thousands lie at the disposal of cops and prosecutors and judges who still think the subject before us is "marital problems." (80)

The American Bar Association (ABA) Commission on Domestic Violence (1997) observes that violence between intimate partners

> has a tremendous impact on the legal profession. Whether or not lawyers realize it, domestic violence permeates the practice of law in almost every field. Corporate lawyers, bankruptcy lawyers, tort lawyers, real property lawyers, criminal defense lawyers, and family lawyers, regularly represent victims of domestic violence. (I-5)

However, the commission also notes that many legal professionals lack understanding of domestic violence and fail to represent victims effectively. Further, the commission suggests that uninformed legal professionals may put victims at risk "or contribute to a society which has historically condoned the abuse of intimate partners" (I-5).

Many batterers rape their female partners, often causing serious physical and psychological damage (Browne 1992; Tjaden and Thoennes 2000; Wiehe and Richards 1995). Despite the well-documented harm inflicted by rape, defining rape within marriage as a crime continues to be controversial. Russell reports,

> A few states have completely eliminated the marital exemption from their law; others have enacted legislation that makes some rapes within marriage a crime; and in other states court actions have essentially overturned the marital exemption. (cited in Crowell and Burgess 1996, 127)

While at present all 50 states and the District of Columbia have repealed the marital rape exemption, definitions of the offense are inconsistent across jurisdictions and where statutes do exit, sanctions vary widely (Bernat 2001; Bergen 1999; Wiehe and Richards 1995). Thirty-three states currently uphold exemptions that protect husbands from rape prosecution, substantiating the view that rape in marriage is a lesser crime than other forms of rape (Bergen 1999). Some states grant husbands "partial exemption" allowing for prosecution only if the couple is separated or obtaining a divorce, but penalties remain relatively low (Doerner and Lab 1998). Marital rape rarely results in prosecution (Caringella-MacDonald 1997) since very few cases ever make it to trial (Mahoney and Williams 1998). Clearly, American law has been slow to label as criminal the actions of men who assault their wives. As a result, abusive men tend to face little punishment for their violence against women and female victims receive little protection from them.

Psychological Abuse

Even more hidden than marital rape, psychological abuse is an essential component of men's control and domination of their female partners. Repeatedly, even women who have been severely injured by husbands describe the psychological, mental, and emotional abuse as more damaging and difficult to overcome than the physical trauma (Foster, Veale, and Fogel 1989). Psychological abuse is part of a process of intimidation enacted to establish and maintain the abuser's control over his wife. Forms of psychological abuse reported by women include threats to kill or harm her and/or the children, threats to kidnap her and/or the children, destruction of property, verbal abuse (Ptacek 1997), isolation/imprisonment, guilt induction, required secrecy, and fear arousal (Andersen, Boulette, and Schwartz 1991). Far from being insignificant, male verbal abuse of female intimates is a clear predictor of domestic violence (Tjaden and Thoennes 2000.)

Browne (1995) likens the relationship between male intimate abusers and their female victims to that of wartime captor and captive:

> Parallels also exist between the principles of brainwashing used on prisoners of war and the experiences of some women in battering relationship . . . [including] isolation of the victim from outside contacts and sources of help, and humiliation and degradation by the captor, followed by acts of kindness coupled with the threat of a return to the degraded state if some type of compliance is not obtained. (239)

Jones (1994) features the following chart (see Table 1) of coercive techniques, created by Amnesty International and adapted by a women's shelter. The list of terrorist techniques originated from descriptions provided by hostages, political prisoners, and concentration camp survivors. Despite the damage done by the psychological, emotional, and mental abuse described, many of these actions do not constitute a crime under current statutes.

Table 1
Methods of Coercion

Method of Coercion	Examples
ISOLATION	
Deprives victim of all social support for ability to resist.	He moved me away from my friends. He didn't want me to go anwhere unless he was with me. He would eavesdrop.
Develops an intense concern with self.	
Makes victim dependent upon interrogator	

(continued)

Table 1 (Continued)

Method of Coercion	Examples
MONOPOLIZATION OF PERCEPTION	
Fixes attention upon imme-diate predicament; fosters introspection. Eliminates stimuli competing with those controlled by captor. Frustrates all actions not con-sistent with compliance.	I was always scared he'd blow up. I had to dress up for him. Give him sex whenever he wanted. I had to control the children so they wouldn't bother him. It was like walking on eggshells.
INDUCED DEBILITY AND EXHAUSTION	
Weakens mental and physical ability to resist.	He wouldn't let me sleep. He started fights at night. He wouldn't let me see a doctor.
THREATS	
Cultivate anxiety and despair.	He threatened to kill the cat. He said he'd take the kids. He said he'd have me committed. He said he'd burn down the house. He said he'd find me if I left.
OCCASIONAL INDULGENCES	
Provide positive motivation for compliance.	He took me on vacation. He bought me jewelry. He allowed me sex only when we "made up." Once in a while he really listened to me and seemed to care.
DEMONSTRATING "OMNIPOTENCE"	
Suggests futility of resistance.	He beat me up. He had me fol-lowed. He called me deluded.
DEGRADATION	
Makes cost of resistance appear more damaging to self-esteem than capitulation. Reduces prisoner to "animal level" concerns.	He told me I'm too fat. He'd call me names and touch me inappropri-ately in public. He put me down in-tellectually and sexually and said I was ugly.
ENFORCING TRIVIAL DEMANDS	
Develops habit of compliance.	The bacon had to be cooked to a par-ticular doneness. I couldn't leave a cup on the bathroom basin.

Source: Amnesty International, *Report on Torture* (1973), as adapted by the women's shelter of Northampton, Massachusetts, and reproduced in Jones (1994) *Next Time She'll Be Dead.*

The Police

Historically, law enforcement policies and procedures provided little relief for battered women (Attorney General's Task Force on Family Violence 1984; Gillespie 1989; Miller 1993; Pleck 1987; Sedlak 1988; U.S. Commission on Civil Rights 1982). Over the past three decades, in response to pressure from women's groups, failure-to-protect lawsuits, national studies, and federal pressure, the policing of domestic violence has shown improvement (Fagan 1996; Ferraro 1993; Friedman and Shulman 1990; Gagne 1998; Sherman 1992). Pro-arrest approaches to domestic assaults have become common policy in many jurisdictions across the country (Caringella-MacDondald 1997; Lattimore et al. 1997; Sherman 1992). Hart (1990b) observes, "Research reveals that arrest is the most effective response of law enforcement to domestic violence" (1). Especially when part of a coordinated community response system, police-initiated interventions are shown to reduce the risk of renewed violence and result in more sanctions for batterers (Jolin et al. 1998).

Nevertheless, despite the pro-arrest policies of many agencies, even when specific actions are defined as illegal and policies mandate particular responses, there is no guarantee that law enforcement personnel will enforce those laws or follow departmental policies with consistency (Belknap 2001; Bourg and Stock 1999; Caringella-MacDonald 1997; Ewing 1997; Gillespie 1989; Miller 1993; O'Dell 1996). Sherman (1992) notes that many officers still fail to define and record domestic violence incidents as crimes. Marvin (1997) reports, "[L]aw enforcement still does not address domestic violence in the same way it addresses other violent crimes" (65) despite the recent progress. Further, batterers who violate civil orders of protection seldom face arrest (Belknap 2001; Caringella-MacDonald 1997; Crowell and Burgess 1996; Gillespie 1989). When police respond to domestic violence with reluctance or indifference, it can be interpreted by the parties involved, their children, and society as a whole as condoning the activity (Crowell and Burgess 1996; Gillespie 1989).

Most women do not report their victimization to police because they believe the police can do nothing about it and because they believe that the police would not believe them (Tjaden and Thoennes 2000). Research on police response to spousal assault reveals that police officers, like the public at large, hold stereotypical views[1] about battered women and family fights that undermine their effectiveness in dealing with the batterer and the victim (Andersen et al.

1991; Ferraro 1989; Gibbs 1997). In addition, law enforcement has long accepted as truth the erroneous concept that domestic violence calls, subsumed in the category "disturbance calls," are the most dangerous calls to the police. However, a closer examination of the FBI numbers contributing to that belief shows that the majority of police killed in disturbance calls were dealing with bar fights rather than domestic violence calls, and the actual number killed in domestic conflict situations was a much smaller proportion, even less than the number of accidental deaths at the hands of fellow officers (Sherman 1988).

In general, the tendency persists for officers to view women claiming to have been abused as noncredible and unworthy of police time (Belknap 1995; Hart 1992). Abel and Suh (1987) report that while 60 percent of the three hundred battered women in their study asked to have their spouses arrested, police arrested the abusers only 28 percent of the time. Victims' requests for arrests were ignored in 75 percent of the cases examined by Buzawa, Austin, and Buzawa (1995). Saunders's (1995) vignette study of police officers' tendency to arrest domestic violence victims found that patriarchal norms and general attitudes about victims were not related to arrest options; however, the likelihood that officers would choose the arrest option was associated with their justification of domestic violence.

Battered women not only face the reluctance of some officers to arrest abusers, they also contend with a growing possibility of their own arrests if they use physical force to defend themselves (Buzawa and Buzawa 1993; Ferraro 1997; Friedman and Shulman 1990). Of women arrested for domestic violence, only about 2 percent are actually the primary physical aggressors (Healey, Smith, and O'Sullivan 1998). Another distressing development in arrests related to domestic violence further lowers women's faith in police intervention: increasingly, battered women are being arrested and charged with failing to protect their children, even fetuses, from exposure to domestic violence (Jacobs 1998; Roth 2000; Schneider 2000; Sengupta 2000).

A National Institute of Justice study of domestic violence (Sherman 1988) recommends that since domestic violence is a crime, police officers are obligated to treat it seriously and to provide protection for the victims, especially victims of repeated assaults. Law enforcement personnel in many jurisdictions have benefited from expanded and revised domestic violence training programs (Hart 1990b; O'Dell 1996; Payne 1996). But Ferraro (1989) observes that changes in law enforcement practices must be accompanied by changes in all levels of the criminal justice system:

> Mandatory and presumptive arrest policies implemented in the absence of change in other parts of the legal system will probably have little lasting impact on how police respond to domestic violence. (72)

Police may be reluctant to bring their full law enforcement power to bear on domestic violence situations due to lack of prosecutorial and judicial support, the low status of the offense as far as professional incentives and rewards are concerned, and perceived lack of follow-through by the victims. According to the Bureau of Justice Assistance, "Without a policy of strong prosecution, efforts by law enforcement agencies have little impact" (Hofford and Harrell 1993).

The Prosecution

The office of the prosecutor, with its broad discretionary powers, serves as gatekeeper to the court system. Historically, prosecutors have been slow to bring charges against men who beat their female partners (Fagan 1996; Hart 1990b; U.S. Commission on Civil Rights 1982) and these historic patterns often reassert themselves (Caringella-MacDonald 1997). Domestic violence cases continue to experience high levels of attrition once they enter the prosecutorial stage (Bowker 1987; Doerner and Lab 1998). Aggressive prosecution policies are being adopted by many jurisdictions (Freidman and Shulman 1990). Problematically, in some districts, a woman who refuses to testify against her partner may be charged with contempt of court and incarcerated (Ferraro 1993).

Prosecution rates vary widely by jurisdiction, and where criminal justice interventions are not supported the rate of prosecution has been low (Crowell and Burgess 1996). In many communities, prosecution rates remain low, less than 10 percent for misdemeanor cases (Fagan 1996). Marcus (1981) cites the unwillingness of district attorneys and judges to prosecute and sentence domestic assailants as an influence in law enforcement decisions.

Buzawa and Buzawa (1996) report that domestic violence crimes often are not treated as seriously as they might deserve in the prosecution process and that, in the limited instances of convictions, sentences are quite lenient. Further, they describe a general bias in the court against relationship cases, which makes them disproportionately vulnerable to settlement or dismissal. Bail is usually not set high enough to keep the abuser in custody until a preliminary hearing. Frequently, following an arrest for spousal assault, a man is released on bail or on his own recognizance almost immediately, allowing him to return home and intimidate or assault his partner. The U.S. Commission on Civil Rights (1982) reports,

> Judges who are indifferent and unwilling to impose any meaningful sanctions on abusive spouses convey a message to both victims and their abusers that the courts will not stop the violence. . . . [T]hey influence police, prosecutors, and other members of the justice system in formulating their own attitudes and policies for handling spouse abuse cases. (59)

In many jurisdictions, prosecution of the batterer is left to the discretion of the victim rather than to the district attorney, leaving her vulnerable to the abuser's threats. Pagelow (1981) notes prosecutorial blindness regarding the special nature of the assailant/injured party relationship: "[V]ictim's fears of retaliation for prosecution is a significant problem when the perpetrator of a crime resides with his victim" (79). Moreover, making the woman responsible for the batterer's prosecution encourages the offender to place the blame for his legal problems on his partner rather than on his own actions. In 1982, the Swedish government recognized the problems inherent in such an arrangement and altered the law so that spousal assault, including non-aggravated assault on private property, is subject to public prosecution whether or not the victim presses the issue (Hyden 1994).

Many prosecutors place obstacles along the way of women who want the full weight of the law brought to bear on their assailants. Waiting periods, for example, discourage battered women from relying on the justice system for safety. Filing lesser charges than those recommended by the police diminishes the victim's trust in the system. Women are seldom fully informed of their civil rights or given extra protection from their violent partners. In cases where the woman has to relocate, the offender's attorney is able to obtain her new address, which gives opportunity for the batterer to discourage her from pressing charges or testifying.

The U.S. Civil Rights Commission found that prosecutors sometimes refuse to prosecute batterers because they expect noncooperation from the victim even when the victim is willing to go ahead with the charges. Many women have complained that prosecutors "fail to vigorously investigate their cases" (Hart 1990b). In Pagelow's (1981) study of 350 women in shelters, none related filing charges that resulted in trial, sentencing, and jail. Zorza (1997) reports that, contrary to the stereotype, battered women are no more likely to want to drop charges than are any other recontacted victims of violent felonies threatened with further abuse. In jurisdictions where prosecutors pay special attention to battering cases, prosecution rates are high (Crowell and Burgess 1996), and the vast majority of injured parties cooperate in the pursuit of prosecution (Marcus 1981). Furthermore, as Zorza (1997) points out,

> The same prosecutors who have refused to go forward without a victim's cooperation when she is alive have no problem prosecuting her abuser without her assistance after the abuser has killed her. (7)

The Judiciary

The court plays a critical role in determining the official response to domestic violence. Judges determine pretrial release conditions, sentences, the existence and amount of bond, and whether or not to issue an order of protection (Crowell and Burgess 1996). Judges exert influence over police and prosecution practices as well as the behaviors of defendants and victims (Goolkasian 1986). The history of judicial response to domestic violence, however, corresponds to that of law enforcement and prosecutors. Leniency with batterers (Bannister 1993; Crowe 1996), dismissed charges (Friedman and Shulman 1990), acceptance of stereotypes of women as emotional and unreliable witnesses, and blaming victims for causing the violence (Hofford and Harrell 1993) are common occurrences in the courtroom.

Adding to the complex relationship between the judiciary and domestic violence cases, courts hear these cases in a variety of settings within a single court system—from civil courts, to family court, to misdemeanor and felony courts. At all levels, courts are overburdened with the volume of domestic abuse cases. Some states have as many as five different courts hearing various kinds of family matters (Hofford and Harrell 1993).

Crites (1987), suggests that a judicial pattern exists that reveals an unwillingness to see wife abuse as a crime and a tendency to side with the husband in domestic violence cases; she cites as further evidence the resistance of judges to issuing orders of protection that temporarily exclude the men from their homes. Some judges may refuse to grant hearings mandated by state law, or may blame the woman for causing the abuse (Marcus 1981). In attempting to press charges against abusers, women have been admonished by the magistrate or judge with comments such as, "If you come back one more time to get a peace warrant, then I will lock you up" (quoted in Foster, Veale, and Fogel 1989, 278).

The ABA Commission on Domestic Violence (1997) report documents further examples of judicial actions that endangered victims:

> In Maryland, for example, a victim was killed by her intimate partner after a judge refused to grant her a civil protection order. Recently, another judge expunged a batterer's criminal record for wife abuse in order to allow him to join a country club; the judge reversed his ruling only in response to public outcry. Still another judge modified a custody order and awarded custody of the child to the child's father, despite the fact that the father had abused the child's mother, and had been convicted of murdering his first wife. (I-5)

The California Committee on Gender Bias in the Courts surveyed 425 judges and found that nearly half believed that allegations of domestic violence are often exaggerated, and some expressed active hostility toward victims of domestic violence. The committee reports,

> Again and again, this committee heard testimony that police officers, district and city attorneys, court personnel, mediators, and judges—the justice system—treated the victims of domestic violence as though their complaints were trivial, exaggerated, or somehow their own fault. (Welling et al. 1990, Sec. 6, 5)

The committee's conclusions include:

1. Some judges and court personnel approach domestic violence cases, whether consciously or unconsciously, with assumptions based not upon personal experience or the facts of a particular case but upon . . . stereotypes and biases . . .

2. Some judges and court personnel lack information about the psychological, economic, and social realities of domestic violence victims.

The committee found that gender bias contributes to the judicial system's failure to afford the protection of the law to victims of domestic violence. (Sec. 6, 5)

As Schafran's (1990) report on gender bias in U.S. courtrooms shows, criminal justice institutions across the nation continue to minimize violence against women and blame the woman for being assaulted:

Domestic violence continues to be an area in which women experience significant bias, despite major statutory reforms to provide them with civil and criminal protections. . . . Instead of focusing on why men batter and what can be done to stop them, many judges and court personnel ask battered women what they did to provoke the violence, subject them to demeaning and sexist comments, shuttle them from court to court, and issue mutual orders of protection when the respondent has not filed a cross-petition and there is no evidence that the petitioner was violent. These women are then castigated for failing to go forward with their cases. (30)

Nevertheless, over the past three decades legislative changes have led to reforms that result in an increase in arrests and requests for restraining orders. Many court systems have had to adjust procedures and processes to accommodate the increase (Hofford and Harrell 1993). While it appears that it is becoming easier for women to obtain restraining orders, violations of these orders are not punished seriously (Schafran 1991). Some districts have established specialized domestic violence courts (McHardy and Hofford 1998) and more jurisdictions are taking into account victim needs and preferences regarding sentencing of offenders (Goolkasian 1986).

At every level, the judiciary has the opportunity to intervene on behalf of women who live in pain and fear of their most intimate partners. Yet, all too often, the courts systematically fail to support and protect the victims, at great cost to the individuals and to society. Each year in America, up to four thousand women are killed by their husbands, boyfriends, or former partners (National Clearinghouse for the Defense of Battered Women 1994); many of them had looked to the courts for help. Stark and Flitcraft (1996) find that on-going assault by male partners "may be the single most important context for female suicide attempts . . ." (120).

The Men Who Die and the Women Who Survive

Some women perceive that every possible escape route away from the terror is closed off from them and the only apparent avenue to end the ongoing violence is through suicide or homicide. A small proportion of abused women end the violence by causing the death of their batterers (Ewing 1987). Research shows that women who kill their abusers tend to do so when they sense no alternative way to protect themselves and/or their children from further harm or death (Browne 1987; Gagne 1998; Jones 1994). Steffensmeier and Allan (1996) concur: "For women to kill, they generally must see their situation as life-threatening, as affecting the physical or emotional well-being of themselves or their children" (480). Contrary to common assumptions, a woman is most likely to use lethal violence against a male partner during an attack on her or her child, not when he is asleep or incapacitated (Maguigan 1991). Clearly, spousal homicide and domestic violence are not disconnected phenomena (Edwards 1985; Moracco et al. 1998).

Researchers and practitioners seek to determine risk factors that differentiate abused women who kill their batterers from those who do not kill. Browne (1987) identifies the following risk factors from her study on women homicide offenders: frequency of violent incidents, severity of injuries, man's threats to kill, woman's threats of suicide, man's drug use, man's frequency of intoxication, and forced sexual acts. Browne also found that 71 percent of the men who were killed had physically and/or sexually abused the children by the end of the relationship. Presence of weapons in the home and the abuser's threats to harm children in the home are cited as additional risk factors (Foster, Veale, and Fogel 1989). Walker (1989) advises,

> Batterers most likely to be killed were the ones who continued to verbally degrade and humiliate a woman while she had a weapon in her hands. So were those men who had sexually abused her or her children. So were those men who ordered the woman to kill them—using her, perhaps to commit their own suicides. (104)

Stark and Flitcraft (1996) cite the level of entrapment, or coercive control, as the single most important risk factor for intimate partner homicides. For the most part, the factors identified by researchers relate to the abuser's actions. Browne (1987) observes, "[F]ew differences can be found in characteristics of the women in the homicide and comparison groups; the differences exist primarily in the behaviors of the men" (127).

Research consistently shows that battering is the most frequent precursor to spousal homicide (Campbell 1995). Frequently, a woman's lethal action is provoked by a sudden change in the pattern of violence, which signals to her that her death is imminent (Browne 1987). Ewing's (1987) summary of several studies on battered women who kill paints a graphic picture of the typical experiences of these women:

> Overall, it seems that the battered woman who kills her batterer has been battered more frequently and has suffered more serious injuries in the course of more rapidly escalating physical abuse. She is more likely to have been raped and sexually abused, threatened with death, and menaced with weapons. Her children are more likely to have been abused by her batterer. She is more likely to live in an environment where a gun is present, and her batterer is more likely to be an alcohol or drug abuser. In addition, it seems that the battered woman who kills may be somewhat older, somewhat less well educated, and more socially isolated than the battered woman who does not kill—characteristics which, coupled with more frequent threats of reprisal for leaving, make it more difficult for her to leave her batterer. (40).

Before the deadly event, many women make repeated but failed attempts to enlist the help of law enforcement for their abusive situations (Browne 1987; Marcus 1981; Moracco et al. 1998; Stout 1991). One study of domestic homicides found that in 85 percent of the cases, the police had been summoned at least one time before the final incident, and in half the cases, the police were called five or more times before the killing occurred (Marcus 1981). Exacerbating the problem, Department of Justice data reveal that police are likely to respond more quickly if the attacker is a stranger than if he is known to the victim (Bachman 1994).

The Criminal Justice Response

The same criminal justice system that often fails to respond to wife abuse seems, in many cases, to prosecute with vigor the battered woman who kills, even though most women offenders of conjugal homicide have no history of criminal or violent behavior (Browne 1987; Leonard 2000; O'Shea 1993; Walker 1989). Wilson (1993) observes,

> Though women kill far less frequently than do men, their actions are less likely to be construed as justifiable by the American legal system, and most probably by the general public. We see this tendency most clearly in two situations: spousal homicide in response to wife battery, and abortion. (49)

Numerous researchers describe gender inequities in the indictment, prosecution, and sentence determination of women who kill their abusers. McCorkel (1996) reports that, historically, women have received longer determinate sentences and have been given indeterminate sentences as well. Chesney-Lind (1995) finds, rather than reflecting a shift in the nature of women's crimes, the dramatic increase in women's incarceration stems from the heightened willingness of the criminal justice system to imprison women. According to Browne (1988), "FBI statistics indicate that fewer men are charged with first or second degree murder for killing a woman they have known than are women who kill a man they have known" (275). Almost without fail, abused women who kill are charged with murder or manslaughter and plead self-defense (Ewing 1990; Osthoff 1991). Ewing's (1990) data on 100 cases in which battered women caused the death of their partners revealed,

> Despite generally abundant evidence that they were severely abused by the men they killed, many if not most of these women are convicted because the circumstances surrounding their homicidal acts do not meet the requirements of current self-defense law. . . . (580)

Moreover, Walker (1992) notes,

> Those who were Black and killed Black or White partners still were twice as likely to have been convicted of murder

and sentenced to longer periods in prison than those who were Caucasian or from other minority groups. Women who were poor and less educated also appeared to have a similar bias against them in the courts. (329)

The Sentences

Women who are found criminally responsible for the death of their abusers rarely receive leniency or compassion (Bannister 1991). In Mann's (1992) random sample of 114 female-perpetrated spousal homicides, more than half of the offenders received prison sentences, with an average of sixteen years to serve. Of the women in Browne's (1987) study, 56 percent argued their cases on the basis of self-defense, 8 percent entered a diminished capacity or insanity plea, and 33 percent pled guilty to a lesser charge in return for leniency in sentencing, and in one case, the charges were dropped; the most common plea arrangement was voluntary manslaughter with reduced jail sentence, or several years probation. The vast majority of women accused of killing their abusive partners (72 percent to 80 percent) are convicted or accept a plea, and many receive long, harsh sentences (Belknap 2001; Gagne 1998; Osthoff 1991). Jones (1996) proposes that when women commit traditionally "masculine" crimes like armed robbery and felony murder, they tend to receive heavier sentences than men convicted for the same offense. Moreover, as Bannister (1993) observes,

> Judges tend to impose lenient sentences on men who are convicted of beating their wives or partners. They do not show the same leniency to women who act in self-defense against their batterers . . . (317).

Stout and Brown (1995) reviewed the sentences of women and men incarcerated in Missouri for killing their partners. Of eighteen women, sixteen had been physically abused by their mates but only five were permitted to present testimony in court about their past abuse; the modal conviction of the female subjects was capital murder, with half of the women (nine) receiving sentences of life without the possibility of parole or life without the possibility of parole for fifty years; four of the women received sentences of life with the possibility of parole; five received sentences of seven to nineteen years. Of the twenty-one men who had killed their spouses, none received sentences of life without the possibility of parole or life without the possibility of parole for fifty years; half of the men were given a life sentence with the possibility of parole; and seven men received sentences ranging from twelve to thirty-five years. Thus, in the Missouri study, the modal sentence for women was strikingly more severe than that for men. Bannister (1991) suggests that male spousal homicide offenders are treated with lenience "because of judges' perceptions that the woman goaded the husband into the act of killing her" (406).

In contrast to much of the literature, Langan and Dawson (1995) report that prison sentences for female spousal homicide offenders averaged ten years shorter than for men. However, they excluded life or death sentences from their averages while finding that wives were not significantly less likely than husbands to receive life sentences. Moreover, four times more wife defendants than husband defendants had been assaulted by their spouse at or around the time of the murder. Their research surveyed cases disposed of in 1988 in thirty-three urban counties and did not include divorced couples. In light of the significant gender differences in the context and consequences of spousal abuse and homicide, comparisons of sentencing patterns for male and female homicide offenses may be of limited utility and may contribute to the misperception that these are inherently equivalent actions.

Frequently, a woman is penalized more harshly because she used a weapon. Research shows that a batterer's primary weapons are his hands, fists, and feet, and that typical battering episodes involve slaps, punches, kicking, stomping, and choking (Gillespie 1989). Beating or strangulation homicides appear to be exclusive to male offenders (Casenave and Zahn 1992). Since men in heterosexual relationships are typically taller, heavier, and stronger than their female partners, few women are able to fend off their attackers without the use of a weapon. Accordingly, Eisenberg and Dillon (1989) suggest that since a woman is merely equalizing the relative strength of females versus males when she uses a weapon, it does not constitute "excessive force," thus, the law should include an "equalizer principle."

The Law and Women's Self-Defense

If, as research shows, women who kill their husbands or lovers most often do so in the context of defending themselves against ongoing violence, why is conviction so common? A number of factors combine to complicate the legal outcomes of what has been termed "homicidal self-help" (Gagne 1998; Jones 1994; Marcus 1981). The actions of defense attorneys, prosecutors, and judges, as well as the law itself, may act to prevent exculpatory information from entering the adjudication process. Sue Osthoff (2001), cofounder and executive director of the National Clearinghouse for the Defense of Battered Women, notes the detrimental persistence of myths and misconceptions about battered women as victims and as defendants that judges, defense attorneys, prosecutors, and jurors bring with them into any trial.

> Generally, the myths and misconceptions that often end up being harmful to battered women charged with crimes have to do with (1) a belief that battered women can and should leave their abusers; (2) a belief that if the woman on trial does not fit the person's stereotype of a battered woman, she is not a "real battered woman"; and (3) a belief in the mutality of abuse (that women are just as violent as, or even more violent than, men). (234)

Stark (1990) reports, "Historically, lawyers defending women who murdered batterers concealed abuse, fearing it would be used against their clients in court" (18). According to Gagne (1998), all too often lawyers who represent women defendants have

> little understanding of the dynamics of wife abuse or the psychological response to chronic violence. . . . Defense attorneys are often unfamiliar with the dynamics of crimes resulting from abuse and know little about defense strategies that could help introduce a defendant's life experiences into evidence. (40, 41)

Defense attorneys may accept cultural myths and stereotypes about battered women,[2] which can distort their legal strategy and advice (Gillespie 1989; Schneider 2000). Batterers typically isolate, humiliate, and terrorize their partners, rendering women's victimization largely hidden from outside others (Gibbs 1997), making it problematic for defense attorneys to produce corroborating evidence of ongoing victimization. As Bannister (1993) points out, women's oppression by society and by abusive partners "leads to an inability to express clearly their account of what happened to their lawyers and/or to the court" (321), which then affects the verdict. Further obscuring the truth, women often find it too painful and humiliating to report their

partners' sexual violence to male defense attorneys, thus creating
further gaps in evidence that could inform defense strategies.

Whether a jurisdiction relies on a prosecutor or a grand jury to
issue a criminal indictment, the prosecutor maintains broad discretion on what charges, if any, to file (Siegel 1998). When prosecutors
choose to charge women for killing abusive partners, they may do so
"in part because they know that they can get juries to convict women
in these circumstances" (Gillespie 1989, 22). If a record of past abuse
by the deceased is admitted into evidence, rather than supporting a
self-defense argument, prosecutors turn it into a motive for the
woman's crime of revenge—she is hysterical and out-of-control or
she is cold-blooded and calculating (Gillespie 1989). Should a homicide occur in a nonconfrontational or preemptive circumstance, such
as hiring someone to kill the man or shooting him while he sleeps
following a prolonged assault or his death threats, prosecutors liken
it to "anarchy" or "open season" on men (Gagne 1998). In explaining
the high rate of convictions, Gillespie (1989) writes,

> The trial courtroom provides a forum for a biased or cynical
> prosecutor to trot out every myth and stereotype and mis-
> conception about women that could conceivably inflame a
> jury against the defendant and that could encourage the ju-
> rors to ascribe the worst possible motive to her actions. (23)

She further argues,

> [A]t the center of virtually every prosecution of a woman's
> self-defense case [is the unspoken assumption] that a
> woman who kills a man with whom she has been intimate
> *must* have had some base and ugly motive for her act, which
> she is subsequently lying about. (25)

A prosecutor's decision as to whether or not criminal charges will be
pursued against someone is influenced by a number of factors, such
as quality of evidence, witness credibility, as well as gender or race
bias; often political interests are a consideration—the electorate expect a "tough on crime" prosecutor (Gillespie 1989).

Trial judges play a pivotal role in the adjudication process. They
decide what evidence will be allowed (including expert testimony or
abuse histories), instruct juries on the rules governing self-defense,
and exercise wide discretion in sentencing. Many judges share with
other members of the criminal justice system and the general public

stereotypic beliefs and biases concerning women and domestic violence (Gillespie 1989), which can influence courtroom decisions. Maguigan (1991) found that many women do not receive fair trials due to "the failure of trial judges to apply the generally applicable standards of self-defense jurisprudence in cases where the defendants are battered women" (437). Moreover, battered women, who have been silenced and intimidated by their abusers, may be rendered silent again by the adversarial nature of the trial setting itself (Schneider 2000; Walker 1989) and by the authoritarian figure of a male judge. Bannister (1993) observes,

> [T]he stark courtroom atmosphere, the neutrality that appears as hostility, with its absence of smiles and lightness and the barking of the judge, all intimidate the women as they testify. (332)

Self-defense law allows a person to use reasonable force against someone when the person believes she is in imminent danger of bodily harm; the level of force must be proportionate to the force used against her; and force is the only means of preventing that harm (Bannister 1993). When a woman's actions fit the legal requirements of self-defense law, she is more likely to be successful in court (Bannister 1991). Castel (1990) argues that the legal requirements for self-defense pleas discriminate against women who kill their abusive partners.
Further,

> The requirements of immediate danger, necessary force, reasonable belief and the duty to retreat present almost insurmountable barriers to a self-defense claim in the wife-battery situation (Wilson 1993, 50).

Expert testimony regarding a defendant's belief that she was in imminent danger when she participated in a nonconfrontational homicide continues to be disallowed in most states (Parrish 1996). Current laws of self-defense are based largely on assumptions that apply best to situations of adult males fighting adult males (Stout 1991) and often do not reflect the reality most battered women experience (Gillespie 1989). Edwards (1985) observes,

> There is undoubtedly a discrepancy between women's everyday reality of the homicide incident and the legal reality into which it must fit or fail since rules relating to homicide

defense as in any other level of jurisdiction have tended to emerge within the context of male oriented law, judiciary and criminology. (196)

The "Syndrome"

Increasingly, attorneys apply the "battered woman syndrome" in their defense of women who kill their abusers (Walker 1992). Battered woman syndrome, as described in the *Diagnostic and Statistical Manual of Mental Disorders, 4th Edition* (American Psychiatric Association 1994), is a subcategory of Post Traumatic Stress Disorder characterized by a pattern of severe physical and psychological abuse inflicted by an abusive mate. This diagnosis is used as a justification defense rather than a mental health defense in most cases (Walker 1987).

Whether or not evidentiary rules allow expert testimony on battered woman syndrome and spousal violence varies by jurisdiction. While expert testimony is now permitted in most states (Gagne 1998), it remains a matter of judicial discretion since only nine states have passed laws specifically permitting expert testimony (Gibbs 1997). Expert witnesses testify about the effect of abuse on women; they give support to a woman's perception that her life was in jeopardy at the time of the homicide; and they show that her actions were reasonable for a person repeatedly subjected to assaults by her husband. Walker (1992) suggests that utilizing the "battered woman's self-defense" allows many more women a fair trial. Appellate courts have ruled that the battered woman syndrome is relevant to a woman's claim of self-defense (Schneider 1986). Nevertheless, even when this type of defense is recognized legally, "[it] may be no warrant against the working perceptions of self-defense applied by traditionally minded judges and juries" (Wilson 1993, 51). Further, while the courts have accepted the concept of "battered woman syndrome," with its related symptom of "learned helplessness," as Jones states,

> [t]hey have whittled the legal understanding of "battered woman" to such a fine point that few living women fit the description. These days, battered women who got angry, or fought back, or called the cops, or took the batterer to court, or bought defensive weapons, or *left*—which is to say, most women who are battered—don't qualify as "helpless." (1994, 103)

In addition, many feminists find problematic the labeling of battered women as "helpless" and the pathologizing of their responses to ongoing abuse as a "syndrome" (e.g., Bowker 1993; Browne 1987; Gagne 1998; Gillespie 1989; Jones 1994; Schneider 1986; 2000). Rather, they argue that women's ongoing survival strategies require a courage and cleverness that refutes the picture of a passive, helpless female. Schneider's (1992) examination of homicide cases involving the battered woman syndrome

> underscored the complexity of the task of expanding defense options for battered women. These cases revealed the tenacity of sex-stereotyping for, despite the purpose for which this legal strategy was conceived, old stereotypes of incapacity were replicated in a new form. Lawyers who submitted testimony focused on the passive, victimized aspects of battered women's experiences, their "learned helplessness," rather than explaining homicide as a woman's necessary choice to save her own life, and judges were hearing the testimony in this way. . . . Judicial and public perceptions of battered woman syndrome as a form of incapacity have had problematic consequences for the defense of battered women who kill and assert self-defense. (561)

The Aftermath

It appears that even when self-defense laws fit the homicide event, lawyers and judges may not apply the laws properly in cases of battered women homicide offenders. Maguigan's (1991) analysis of 223 appellate cases of battered women who killed reveals that approximately 40 percent of the cases were overturned, a rate five times higher than other criminal convictions. Why the remarkably high rate of turnovers? Maguigan reports that many judges refuse to apply the law fairly to battered women defendants, and that trial and appellate attorneys are waiving or failing to pursue reversible or appealable errors on the part of trial judges.

While none of the Missouri women in the Stout and Brown (1995) study received a death sentence, women are more likely than men to be sentenced to death on a first offense (O'Shea 1993) and their numbers are growing. Rapaport (1994) records gender differences in patterns of capital sentencing of domestic killers: "almost half the men killed in retaliation for a woman's leaving a sexual relationship, while this pattern was quite rare among the women. . . ." (225). Dingerson (1991) points out that, among the thirty-four women on U.S. death rows in 1991, several were there for killing their battering partners. Of the thirty-nine women on death row in 1992 as recounted by Streib (1992, 182), "nearly one-half of these cases involved the murder of the offender's husband or lover, surprisingly high at least compared to what we know about the victims of males on death row." By 1993, seventeen states housed forty-five women on death row, 40 percent of whom are black; almost half of the women have a history of abuse and are there for the murder of an abusive spouse or lover (O'Shea 1993). By December 31, 2000, the number of condemned women had increased to fifty-three (Streib 2001).

Pathways to Freedom

Parole, a form of supervised release, becomes a correctional option for prisoners with indeterminate sentences who have served the minimum time stipulated by sentencing guidelines. (Obviously, a sentence of life without the possibility of parole renders an inmate ineligible for parole.) In most states, parole is at the broad discretion of a commission or board appointed by the governor (Clear and Cole 1997). Current trends, however, appear to reduce the likelihood of release for convicted battered women with indeterminate sentences. Currie (1998) notes that

> the average prison time served per violent crime in the United States roughly tripled between 1975 and 1989 (and it has increased even further since)—mainly because offenders were more likely to be imprisoned at all once convicted, partly because many of them stayed behind bars longer once sentenced. (14)

Since the mid-1970s, rates of discretionary parole release have declined:

> In 1977, the majority of those discharged from prison (about 72%) were released as a result of a parole board's discretion. But by 1995 discretionary parole accounted for only half of state prison releases. (Stinchcombe and Fox 1999, 423)

In 1998, the nation's prison population grew 4.8 percent (Beck and Mumola 1999) while the parole population increased by only

1.5 percent (Bonczar and Glaze 1999). Some states have discontinued parole (Ohio and Wisconsin) and some have abolished it for violent offenders (Slambrouck 2000). Others, by refusing to grant parole, have virtually nullified the program. For example, currently, California has more than four thousand inmates who have served the minimum time required to be eligible for parole release but, based on current and future caseload and parole board decision-making processes, it is estimated that an additional five hundred inmates per year will be added to that number (Hargreaves 2000). Even in the rare event that California's Board of Prison Terms grants a parole date, the governor has blocked it—of two thousand cases reviewed, eighteen inmates have been recommended for parole and Governor Gray Davis has refused approval for all of them (Slambrouck 2000). An exception to this pattern occurred on December 7, 2000 when Davis allowed the parole of Rose Ann Parker (Coronado 2000), a participant in the current study. Since then, he has rescinded the parole recommendations of several more convicted survivors. Thus, convicted battered women homicide offenders with indeterminate sentences, especially those in California, have little hope for release on parole.

Recognizing the plight of incarcerated battered women, legal activists in at least thirty-four states have organized to seek relief from the undue harshness of sentencing decisions or mistakes made in adjudication. The goal of this grassroots movement is to gain the release of convicted survivors through gubernatorial clemency (Gagne 1998). Clemency includes commutation—a sentence reduction that may include immediate release based on time served—pardon—a release from incarceration and repeal of conviction—and reprieve—a delay of the penalty, such as execution. Beginning in 1990 with Ohio governor Richard F. Celeste's mass clemency for twenty-five women (Gagne 1998), governors in more than twenty-two states have granted executive clemency to more than 150 women serving sentences for killing or assaulting abusive partners (Kandel and Theisen 1998). However, not all strategies for clemency have been equally successful. Of thirty-four clemency petitions filed in 1992, California Governor Pete Wilson granted only two (a seventy-eight-year-old grandmother released because of "poor health" and one petitioner's sentence reduced from fifteen years-to-life to twelve years-to life with a recommendation for future parole approval) while many failed to receive any response from their petitions (Kandel and Theisen 1998). Documenting the history of the clemency movement, Gagne (1998) finds,

In every state, the success or failure of clemency was dependent upon the political-opportunity structure. Inmates and activists can do everything right, but if authorities will not listen or if they have too much to lose by granting clemency, activists have little choice but to reframe their demands and work to elect more sympathetic officials. (130)

The Prisoners

The actual number of women serving sentences for killing their abusers is not known since, as noted earlier, there is a lack of hard data on women homicide victims or offenders. Current estimates of how many women are in prison for the death of their violent male partners range from eight hundred to two thousand (National Clearinghouse for the Defense of Battered Women 1994). As of 1999, there were 87,199 women prisoners, 11,692 of them in California (Beck 2000). In a recent study of federal and state correctional populations (Harlow 1999), women inmates and probationers report high levels of physical or sexual abuse prior to their current sentence: 40 percent to 57.2 percent of females compared to 9 percent to 16 percent of males; women report current or former male intimate partners to be the most common abusers (up to 66 percent) while men report current or former female intimates to be the least likely abusers of men (3 percent to 6.5 percent). Harlow also reports that 34 percent of abused women were in prison for a violent offense.

Homicide offenders represented about 12 percent of female state and federal prison inmates in 1998 (Greenfeld and Snell 1999). While not all homicides by women are related to domestic violence (Brownstein et al. 1994), between 40 percent to 93 percent of female perpetrated spousal homicides involve the killing of an abusive mate (Browne 1987; Campbell 1992; Totman 1978; Wolfgang 1967). Combining and extrapolating from these estimates and real numbers suggests the number of women in prison for the death of their abusers may be substantially higher than previously thought. Using the more conservative numbers, 12 percent of the midyear 2000 female prison population of 92,688 (Beck and Karberg 2001) indicates 11,123 possible homicide offenders; 40 percent of which suggests the possibility that approximately 4,500 women may be serving prison sentences for the death of abusive male partners.

The current research is unique in its focus on convicted survivors of severe intimate violence. Previous studies have focused on female homicide offenders rather than on battered women who killed (Chimbos 1978, Totman 1978). Browne (1987) examined the lives and cases of forty-five battered women on trial for murder whose cases had a variety of outcomes, including nonincarceration. This is the first study of its size to survey and to conduct an in-depth examination of women in prison for the death of their abusive male partners.

The women who participated in this project have been rendered invisible—first by being female in a male-dominated society; secondly by the social isolation imposed by their abusers and the shame women feel as a result of ongoing victimization; thirdly by the criminal justice sanction for causing the death of their batterers. This study combines quantitative and qualitative data to provide a comprehensive examination of the private lives and legal experiences of women who killed to survive. With the use of surveys and in-depth interviews, it is singular in its breadth and depth of material. This research creates a profile of these women that allows a direct comparison with the general population of California women prisoners. Narratives reveal patterns and processes common to battered women in general and to those who are forced into a deadly confrontation. Analysis of the data suggests improvements and changes in the responses and policies of various social control agencies and intervention systems.

Chapter Three

~

Explaining Intimate Violence:
Theoretical and
Methodological Framework

Theoretical Framework

Despite such gender neutral terms as "domestic violence," "family violence," "partner abuse," and "spouse abuse," hospital records, law enforcement reports, court proceedings, victim surveys, and the historical record consistently show that violence between intimate partners is primarily and essentially the violence of men against women. The battering of women by their male partners occurs more often than any other type of family violence (Levinson 1989; Rasche 1990). Thus, social scientific theories that view intimate abuse as gender neutral (e.g., culture of violence theory [Straus, Gelles, and Steinmetz 1980]; general systems theory [Straus 1980]; resource theory [Goode 1971]; exchange theory [Gelles 1983]; and economic or social stress model [Gelles 1974]) obscure the fundamentally gender specific nature of male violence against wives, fiancées, and girlfriends. Stark and Flitcraft (1996) call attention to

> the deliberate, sexual, and familial dimensions of abuse . . . in the predominance of central injuries to the body, the chest, the breast and the abdomen and by the high rate of violence during pregnancy. (11)

Gender neutral theories assume an equality of power in male-female relationships, a point of view that ignores centuries of male-dominated social systems and structures. Social policies and norms, laws, and physical strength systematically grant men more power than women.
　Historically, religion, law, traditional family structure, the economy, and other social institutions have supported the authority of

39

men over women. As Martin (1983) notes, "The historical roots of our patriarchal family models are ancient and deep" (26). Dobash and Dobash (1979) concur:

> The seeds of wife beating lie in the subordination of females and in their subjection to male authority and control. The relationship between women and men has been institutionalized in the structure of the patriarchal family and is supported by the economic and political institutions and by a belief system, including a religious one, that makes such relationships seem natural, morally just and sacred. (33–34)

Feminists view patriarchal institutions as the source of the structural social control of women by men. They argue that woman battering has more in common with other forms of violence that target women, such as sexual harassment, rape, and incest, than with other forms of family violence, such as elder abuse, sibling abuse, and child abuse (Kurz 1993). Male domination of women continues to be widespread in the United States and around the world, occurring across socioeconomic groups, as well as ethnic, religious, and age groups. According to UNICEF (2000),

> Violence against women and girls continues to be a global epidemic that kills, tortures, and maims—physically, psychologically, sexually and economically. It is one of the most pervasive of human rights violations, denying women and girls equality, security, dignity, self-worth, and their right to enjoy fundamental freedoms.
>
> Violence against women is present in every country, cutting across boundaries of culture, class, education, income, ethnicity and age. (2)

In most countries, rape and sexual abuse by intimates is not considered a crime and women victims often do not view forced sex with a husband or cohabitant as rape (UNICEF 2000). American legal reforms notwithstanding, forced sex (rape) in marriage is not considered much of a crime, further evidence that male-structured laws continue to view women as the property of men within marriage (Andersen 2000). Violence between intimates, therefore, is analyzed most effectively within the context of the gender and power relations that patriarchy generates. Andersen (2000) observes that "radical feminism has produced some of the best explanations of and solutions to high rates of violence against women" (348). Levinson's (1989) cross-cultural examination of family violence in ninety societies demonstrates the clear link between gender inequality and interpersonal violence:

> In general, it seems that in societies without family violence, husbands and wives share in domestic decision making, wives have some control over the fruits of family labor, wives can divorce their husbands as easily as their husbands can divorce them, marriage is monogamous, there is no premarital sex double standard, divorce is relatively infrequent, husbands and wives sleep together, men resolve disputes with other men peacefully, and intervention in wife beating incidents tends to be immediate. (103)

Gender specific violence is a major social and health problem for women globally. Heise's (1994) summary of thirty-five studies from twenty-four countries reveals from one-fourth to more than one-half the women report physical abuse and even more report ongoing emotional and psychological abuse. Most of these studies used probability samples with a large number of respondents from a wide variety of countries. The following quotes from this report demonstrate the pervasiveness of patriarchal attitudes and the oppression of women across time, cultures, and nations (cited in Heise 1994):

> "Wife beating is an accepted custom . . . we are wasting our time debating the issue."

> Comment made by parliamentarian during floor debates on wife beating in Papua New Guinea. (1987)

> "A wife married is like a pony bought; I'll ride her and whip her as I like."

> Chinese proverb

> "Women should wear *purdah* [head-to-toe covering] to ensure that innocent men do not get unnecessarily excited by women's bodies and are not unconsciously forced into becoming rapists. If women do not want to fall prey to such men, they should take the necessary precautions instead of forever blaming the men."

Comment made by a parliamentarian of the ruling Barisan National Party during floor debates on reform of rape laws in Malaysia. (1991)

"The boys never meant any harm to the girls. They just wanted to rape."

Statement by the deputy principal of St. Kizito's boarding school in Kenya after seventy-one girls were raped and nineteen others died in an attack by boys in the school ascribed to the girls' refusal to join them in a strike against the school's headmaster. (1991)

"The child was sexually aggressive."

Justification given by a judge in British Columbia, Canada, for suspending the sentence of a thirty-three-year-old man who had sexually assaulted a three-year-old girl. (1991)

"Are you a virgin? If you are not a virgin, why do you complain? This is normal."

Response by the assistant to the public prosecutor in Peru when a female nursing student reported being sexually molested by police officers while in custody. (1993)

While the feminist framework includes diverse theories, ideas, and programs for change (Andersen 2000), they share basic tenets. Feminists focus on the conditions in society that create and sustain men's power over women. These conditions result from social, not biological, factors. A feminist perspective sees patriarchy as a historical fact and considers gender relations to be the fundamental source of oppression for women. The feminist approach to family violence examines the phenomenon from a macrolevel perspective and emphasizes aspects within the social structure that make the oppression of women and girls endemic to many societies. From this perspective wife beating is a social and political rather than private event—an expression of male privilege rather than individual psychopathology. Supported by institutional norms, men use violence against their wives as an expression of their authority and power and as a reminder to women of their relative subordination and powerlessness. In an analysis of in-depth interviews with abused women and their abusive male partners, Lundgren (1995) exposes the men's "clear strategy" for short and long-term control:

[T]he man acquires control of the woman he lives with. . . . From my interviews with the women, it is frighteningly clear what happens here is extensive, far-reaching control, which means that the man *defines the norms and determines the limits* and boundaries of positive and negative femininity, and that the woman gradually internalizes them. (243–244;, emphasis in original)

Rather than ask the most commonly heard question that arises in regard to battering, "Why doesn't she leave?" or "Why does she stay?," feminists argue that the relevant question is: "Why do men beat their wives?" Feminists point out that questioning the woman's behavior shifts the focus and the blame away from the violent man and onto the victimized woman. A feminist analysis reveals the similarities in the situations, experiences, and dynamics of hostage-captor and female victim-male abuser relationships (Browne 1995; Graham, Rawlings, and Rimini 1990; Jones 1994; Marcus 1994). Marcus (1994) interprets woman battering as a political act—a particular form of terrorism:

There are strong and striking parallels and similarities between terrorism as a strategy used to destabilize a community or society consisting both of women and men, and the abuse and violence perpetrated against women in intimate or partnering situations. Like terror directed at a community, violence against women is designed to maintain domination and control, to enhance or reinforce advantages, and to defend privileges. . . . Whether the violence is identified as the imposition of discipline, as a strategy of family governance, or as an act of masculinity, the consequences are the same. Women learn that they can be kept in their culturally and socially designated "place" by the threat or imposition of physical injury. (32)

Feminist theory and practice reflect the following basic tenets (Bograd 1984):

1. male/female relationships are socially constructed on an unequal distribution of gender-based power;
2. men have differential access to society's valued material and symbolic resources;
3. women are devalued;

4. violence is the most visible form of male control over females;
5. no woman deserves to be abused; and
6. men, not their female partners, are responsible for their actions.

The patriarchal legacy recreates patterns of male domination through socialization, through a gendered division of labor inside and outside the home, and through social institutions that seem to support a man's right to control "his" woman. The *man* is to "wear the pants in the family"; the home is *his* "castle"; the *man* is the head of the household; the wife is to "love, honor, and *obey*" her husband. Wage inequality persists, with women earning only 74 percent of men's earnings (Andersen 2000). Ptacek (1990) suggests that when "police officers and judges encounter batterers, a mutual validation of victim-blaming and minimization occurs" (155). Studies that specifically examine gender bias in the courtroom show that the judicial system continues to minimize the violence of husbands against wives and often places the blame for the abuse on the women victims (Schafran 1990; Welling et al. 1990).

Women's Self-Defense

Not all homicides are punished. The law takes into account killing to protect one's life, the life of another, or in defense of one's property (Schneider, Jordan, and Arguedas 1981). Self-defense law allows for the use of a "reasonable" level of force, which Gagne (1998) describes "as the least amount necessary to repel the assailant, considering the level of danger posed and the available means of deterrence" (24–25). However, Castel (1990) finds that the legal requirements for a successful self-defense discriminate against battered women who kill their abusers. When a woman uses lethal force against an abusive husband or boyfriend, she encounters the full weight of the patriarchal patterns that persist in the criminal justice system. Laws embody masculine assumptions about what circumstances and actions make a homicide justifiable or self-defensive: (1) the antagonists are men of relatively equal strength and fighting ability; and (2) the antagonists were strangers or non-intimates and the situation allowed one of them to withdraw, unless the attack was so sudden that retreat was impossible (Gillespie 1989). These male-patterned qualifications do not fit the typical case of a woman who kills her abuser. She is not likely to be as strong as her husband who is certainly not a stranger to her, nor is his violence an isolated incident from which she can withdraw easily. Along with the gender bias influencing judges, lawyers, and jurors (including female judges, lawyers, and jurors), gender insensitive laws represent factors that combine to place women defendants in an unfair position before the law (Gillespie 1989).

A woman who defends herself against male violence defies the cultural myths and ideals of womanhood: women give life; they do not take a life; women are passive and in need of male protection; a woman who kills her mate is either sick or criminally deviant. A battered woman who claims that the homicide was justified based on self-defense challenges too many norms—after all, "she could have left anytime she wanted to." The fact that a woman uses a gun or knife to protect herself from a deadly assault by an "unarmed" man allows the law to view her use of a weapon as an act of retaliation with unnecessary force. The law frequently does not take into account that a man's most common weapons are his hands, fists, and feet as he chokes, kicks, punches, beats her, and tries to kill her with his hands, fists, or feet.

In some cases women commit the homicide after the man has passed out or gone to sleep, a circumstance even farther removed from masculine legal assumptions. A "real man" faces his foe in a fair fight and does not lie in wait and ambush his victim "like a coward." The "appropriate" situation for using deadly force in self-defense simply does not fit the lived experiences of battered women. The only means many women have with which to defend themselves is to catch their assailants off-guard. A woman whose intimate assailant has injured her, terrorized her, held her hostage, and threatened to kill her and/or her children knows firsthand what is likely to happen when he awakens. Her fear stems from past experiences and it is a reasonable fear.

The law, however, requires juries to apply the "reasonable person" ("reasonable man," until recently) standard to a woman's behavior. While the law is designed to consider the impact of danger and fear on an individual's perception of the situation, Schneider, Jordan, and Arguedas (1981) note,

> The law of self-defense does not take into account women's perspectives and the circumstances under which women are forced to respond. . . . Views of self-defense which prevent the woman's actions from appearing as reasonable as a

man's must be eliminated from the trial process. . . . Sex bias permeates the legal doctrine regarding the perception of imminent and lethal danger. (8)

Gillespie (1989) explains how women are penalized in two ways with the use of an objective standard of reasonableness. The reasonable man/reasonable person test

> causes women's actions to be judged by an inappropriate masculine yardstick. In addition, it is often the basis of trial courts' refusing to admit expert testimony in cases involving battered women on the ground that testimony about the defendant's subjective perceptions is irrelevant to the question of whether a theoretical reasonable person would have acted as she did. (189)

Schneider (1992) suggests that the problem of reasonableness must be understood in the broader context of women's subordination. In elucidating the dilemmas faced by lawyers who attempt to educate judges and juries about male battering and female self-defense, she cautions that the emphasis on the unique characteristics of battered women's experiences may "penalize women's different experiences and women's departures from a stereotypical norm" (1992, 566). Pioneers in research on the link between female injury and domestic violence as well as abuse in medical settings, Evan Stark and Anne Flitcraft (1996) state,

> The medical, psychiatric, and behavioral problems presented by battered women arise because male strategies of coercion, isolation, and control converge with discriminatory structures and institutional practices to make it difficult, sometimes impossible, for women to escape from abusive relationships when they most want to or need to. (xx)

The tenacity of patriarchal patterns obscures the linkage between the problems faced by battered women and women's overall subordinate position within society. Societal patterns that disfavor women, whether cultural or institutional (e.g., family structure, economic and political relations, religious and educational arrangements, and legal systems) perpetuate and legitimize violence against women.

Methodological Framework

This study is guided by a feminist epistemology that supports the voices of women and seeks to give greater visibility to women's experiences. Bergen (1993) observes, "[B]y starting with the private experiences of women, feminists explore how 'personal' problems are the result of structured gender inequality" (200). Fundamental to feminism is the belief that women are experts of their own lives and, therefore, must be part of the research process. As female voices articulate particular and individual stories, they combine to articulate broader societal patterns that reflect patriarchal social institutions and patterns. A woman's personal experience is embedded in a multilayered social reality—a reality formed and influenced by gender subordination at the interpersonal, family, community, institutional, and societal levels.

While there is no one feminist method (Murphy and O'Leary 1994), feminist domestic violence researchers often use and encourage qualitative methods based on the ethos that the real life situations of formerly battered women are best described by the women themselves (Yllo and Bograd 1988). Within this framework, the researcher desires to delve deeply into the social context of abused women's lives in order to portray more accurately their texture and reality. This sociological method of inquiry takes "the standpoint of women" as described by Dorothy Smith (1992). Further, feminists argue that when both researcher and researched are women, their shared gender experience results in a greater willingness on the part of subjects to share their thoughts and lives (Renzetti and Lee 1993).

Neuman (1994) describes the feminist researcher as one who (1) interacts and collaborates with her subjects; (2) uses multiple methods, often qualitative research and case studies; and (3) creates social connections and builds a trusting social relationship. Because feminist principles frame women as experts of their own lives, this research gives voice to women prisoners who met deadly violence with deadly violence. Asking women about their private lives, especially their relationships with violent men and the subsequent homicide, means probing into intimate and painful personal areas. To be admitted into the lives of convicted survivors requires a particular relationship of trust between researcher and researched that must be constructed prior to the interview process.

Domestic violence is a sensitive topic, and causing the death of one's abusive spouse is even more sensitive. Revisiting and speaking about traumatic experiences is emotionally costly for a woman and raises the potential for her to reexperience terror and shame. Accordingly, Edwards (1993) cautions,

> Some of those writing about in-depth interviewing on sensitive subjects express concern about the way this type of interaction can upset and cause emotional harm to those interviewed. . . . At its most extreme, after an interview the subject may be left with her emotional life in pieces and no one to help put them back together . . . (192)

According to feminist criminologists Kathleen Daly and Meda Chesney-Lind (1988),"The victimization (and survivorship) of women is a large and growing part of criminology and is of central interest to feminists in and outside criminology" (520). They also point to the link between victimization and offending, especially among women. With its theoretical and methodological strengths and sensitivities, a feminist framework is likely to provide a more accurate depiction of how battered women become involved in homicide. Thus, this perspective is appropriate for examining the lives of battered female homicide offenders.

Chapter Four

~

Study Format and Design

Introduction

No one knows how many women serve prison sentences for the death of their abusive male partners. A large part of the problem is that not all criminal justice systems collect systematic data on victim-offender relationships in homicide cases. The inmate correctional files of battered women often do not contain data on abusive victim-offender relations. In addition, because court proceedings might not include information on abuse patterns in cases of battered women who kill, the adjudication process is an unreliable source for the identification of such cases. Complicating the situation still further, formerly abused incarcerated homicide offenders may not self-identify as abused women, nor share their histories with others. Thus, it is not possible to locate and select a random sample of this population for study.

Bordering on invisible, incarcerated battered women represent a highly disenfranchised and vulnerable segment of our society. Clearly, research is required to determine the size of the prison population of women who have killed their abusers, their profile, and their sentences. Information is needed on the patterns of responses by social control agencies to the women's past violent victimization at the hands of male partners. Goetting (1995) recommends the collection of in-depth interviews with incarcerated women to elicit from them "the more personal dynamics of their violent behavior" (53). Brownstein et al. (1994) call for further qualitative research in order to understand more clearly the circumstances and characteristics of homicides committed by females. Chesney-Lind (1986) observes,

> Much more basic research must be undertaken on the character and extensiveness of women's deviance and on the

49

motives expressed by . . . criminal women before a theory or
theories of women's lawbreaking can be developed. . . . Books
that are based on in-depth interviews with women in the
[criminal justice] system also provide important sources of
information on women offenders' perceptions of their behavior and their options. (86, 87)

Research Design

To address some of the gaps in knowledge regarding female spousal
homicide offenders, this study utilizes quantitative and qualitative
methods to explore and describe women incarcerated at one California state prison for the death of abusive partners. The study begins
the process of determining the number of women at this institution
who killed violent partners and compares them with the general
population of California women inmates. This work identifies patterns and processes common to this sample and addresses policy issues arising from the women's accounts of their experiences of
victimization and violent self-defense.

Access to potential study participants required a lengthy and
precise process of approval across multiple institutions. In March
1995, I began seeking project approval from the University of California, Riverside Human Subjects Review Committee (HSRC); the
California Department of Corrections (CDC), Research Branch; the
California Institution for Women, Frontera (CIW); and Convicted
Women Against Abuse (CWAA), an inmate-led support group for battered women at CIW. After meeting all requirements mandated by
HSRC, CDC, and CIW, and with permission from the CWAA mem-
bership of approximately fifty-five women, many of whom serve sentences for the death of their abusers, I attended my first support
group meeting in October 1995. Averaging two times per month,
CWAA members meet for two hours of semi-structured, inmate-led
group interaction.

Wife battering and intimate homicide are very personal and del-
icate areas for a researcher to explore. Thus, and in keeping with
feminist research principles, I did not immediately seek interviewees
from the group; rather, I began my relationship with the group by in-
troducing the research project and myself stating, "I am here to learn
from all of you." The women warmly welcomed me and expressed
support for the focus of the study, women convicted for the death of

their male abusers. During the six months that preceded the interview portion of the study, I observed, listened, asked an occasional question, and participated in small group activities. The practice of reciprocity in research, in accord with feminist principles, reduces the asymmetry of the research process among individuals who lack societal resources, rights, and power (Hondagneu-Sotelo 1996). The women of CWAA responded with openness and soon treated me as any other woman—more as a member than as a researcher. Deference gave way quickly to democracy as I, like others, waited my turn on the "talk list" to ask questions or make comments.

CWAA soon revealed itself as more than a self-help or support group for its members with discussion of family violence in general and a woman's personal experience in particular. Members also use the gathering to share current news events regarding battered women, homicide cases, and pertinent court rulings. Women share their experiences with the criminal justice system and discuss possible legal strategies to affect their potential release. In the past, representatives from various media have visited the group and stories emerged on the efforts of lawyers and inmates to seek clemency for incarcerated battered women. Group members continue to monitor media for stories or for journalists with a focus on domestic violence.

My pre-interview education by the group sensitized me to the women's past, present, and future life conditions. I observed that most were able to talk about their trials and many were able to share bits and pieces of abusive and frightening interactions with their partners. However, I soon realized that most, if not all, the members convicted of murder were reluctant or unable to discuss the painful and traumatic homicide event. In one instance, a woman tearfully asked others to suggest ways to help her recall the deadly interaction before her case came up for review by the parole board—her decade-old memories remaining clouded, confusing, and painful.

When ready to begin interviewing, I passed around a signup sheet during a group meeting, asking members to sign if they were incarcerated for the death of male abusers and to indicate whether or not they were willing to be interviewed. That first evening, twenty-six prisoners identified themselves as women who killed to survive an abusive partner and volunteered for interviews. Ensuing nights produced more interviewees and cases. Early participants shared information about my research project with other groups and individuals. After her interview, one woman posted a copy of the informed consent statement (see Appendix A) in her housing unit to help locate other battered women prisoners for the study. CWAA members identified eight non-member inmates (with their permission) with cases that appeared to fit the focus of my research.

A random sample of formerly battered women incarcerated by the state for the death of their abusers is not possible since systematic data on such cases do not exist. Rather, the forty-two interviewees in this study were self-selected through a combination of purposive and snowball sampling. Women interviewed do not represent the general population of incarcerated female spousal homicide offenders in the United States nor the general population of incarcerated female spousal homicide offenders at CIW. Therefore, this exploratory study and its results are not representative of all spousal homicide cases involving battered women. Nevertheless, with a robust sample of forty-two, this is the largest and most representative study to date that examines women in prison for the death of their intimate male abusers

A number of women expressed the expectation that participation in the study would help address the social injustices that contribute to domestic violence as well as to unjust incarcerations. Several felt that it would be a personally beneficial experience to talk in confidentiality about their lives with an interested outside party. One CWAA member whose abuser was injured but not killed expressed regret at not being able to contribute to the study. Thus, based on her interest, her outspokenness in the group, and the similarity of her case to my research focus, I selected her to pre-test the survey questionnaire and the open-ended interview schedule. She suggested that questions not be changed, but that I should allow a full three hours for each interview and to limit interviews to two interviews per day. I followed her advice and arranged with prison staff for interviews to begin.

Ultimately, forty-five women were interviewed, but three cases did not fit the focus of my research. While an abusive male partner was part of each woman's crime, in two cases the homicide victim was not the abuser, and in the remaining case, the woman was convicted of attempted homicide. Two additional women who were convicted for the death of their spouses declined to be interviewed and a third woman was terminally ill with cancer and unable to participate. In sum, this research has identified forty-five cases of abused women at one California prison who killed their violent partners and collected data from forty-two of these women.

The Interview Instruments

This research uses three different data collection techniques—a triangulation of in-depth interviews, questionnaires, and participant observation. Bloom (1996) provides a detailed description of the California female prisoner population drawn from interviews with a random sample of 294 women incarcerated in four California state prisons. The 208-question survey instrument used to develop Bloom's prisoner profile was modified for this study in order to develop a preliminary profile of incarcerated female spousal homicide offenders and to compare key characteristics of this group with the overall female prison population in California. A particular strength of the current study is the direct comparison it is able to make between women prisoners within the same state using equivalent survey instruments. It was in my capacity as a member of Owen and Bloom's (1995) research team that I first encountered women imprisoned for the death of abusive partners and, at that time, determined to conduct research on the topic.

Interviews began with the questionnaire (see Appendix B), then advanced to qualitative, in-depth questions (see Appendix C). I filled out the questionnaire as women responded to survey questions. Interestingly, the questionnaire seemed to serve as an icebreaker and as a link to the more personal and involved qualitative portion of the interview. In-depth, open-ended questions comprised the bulk of the interview period during which the women were asked to talk about: (1) Childhood experiences in their family of origin; (2) Their first experience of abuse, either as children, teenagers, or adults, and their responses to that abuse; (3) Previous marriages or abusive relationships; (4) The violent relationship with the deceased batterer, including the reactions of others who knew about the abuse; (5) Their strategies for controlling, ending, or escaping the violence; (6) The batterer's violence toward others; (7) Outside interventions; (8) The homicide event; (9) Criminal justice response to the homicide; (10) Jail experiences, trials, and plea bargains; (11) Life behind bars; (12) Self-definitions; (13) Advice for currently battered women; and (14) Events, decisions, or interventions that might have affected the final outcome of death and incarceration. A second, follow-up questionnaire was administered via mail.

Interviews took place, depending upon availability, in various private offices located in a prison administration building. In a few instances, outside noise from maintenance or repair of the building and prison grounds would render parts of the audiotape unintelligible. Interviews took place over a three-month period and ranged in duration from one and one-half to three hours, with most lasting the full three hours. For the comfort of the women, I provided tissues and fresh bottled water, and I rearranged office furniture in an attempt to form a conversational, nonhierarchical setting for interaction. Interviews began with an explanation of procedures and an opportunity for each individual to ask questions about the interview process, the study, and the researcher. Each respondent signed an informed consent statement for the interview and its tape recording.

The women experienced a wide range of emotion as we spoke. Some shifted back and forth from visible distress to seeming detachment. Others began in a particular emotional frame and stayed largely within that emotion throughout the interaction. At times a woman would be clearly upset as she recounted specific episodes and welcomed offerings of tissue, water, and empathy. Almost without fail, women appeared to leave the interview in a more positive mood than they showed at the onset of the interaction. Many interviewees openly expressed gratitude for the freedom to tell "the whole story" to someone with whom they felt comfortable. A surprisingly large proportion of the women stated that this was their first opportunity to freely tell their stories, to express their lives, their abusive experiences, and their perceptions. Constructing their stories from beginning to end seemed to provide many women with a greater sense of relatedness among events where, previously, they had not seen clear connections. The forty-two women who participated in this study are unique individuals whose generosity and openness contribute to our understanding of battered women who defend their lives with deadly force.

One woman entered the interview room and froze at the sight of the tape recorder, clearly frightened. I reassured her that she had control over what, if anything, of our conversation would be taped. Still standing, she spoke of what the tape recorder symbolized to her and how the prosecution used it against her during trial. We decided to proceed with the survey portion of the interview after which we would gauge her willingness to move onto the in-depth questions. The woman's confidence appeared to grow as we carefully made our way through the questionnaire. Upon finishing the survey questions, I suggested four options for her to consider: (1) decline the remainder of the interview; (2) allow me to take written notes without recording on tape; (3) control the tape machine herself, turning it off and on with particular questions and responses; or (4) permit the tape machine to record all of the remaining interview. She determined that, by giving permission for the tape recorder to run unhindered, she would regain the power lost through the trial process and the tape recorder would then lose its power to frighten and intimidate her. She completed the full interview and left the room expressing a sense of pride in her accomplishment.

Most women were able to discuss their experiences with candor and increasing ease as the interview process unfolded. Because this study is based largely on the subjective accounts of women in prison, questions are likely to arise regarding the credibility of their stories. During the extended period of participant observation prior to the interviews, I had the opportunity to listen to many future interviewees discuss their lives. I found that interview material, while substantially more detailed and in-depth, was consistent with information gathered in the participant observation process. Over time, a relationship of trust developed between us—researcher and researched. As a consequence, women were even less likely to present false information to me, a person with whom they had developed an ongoing relationship. Moreover, at the close of each interview, I sought consent from respondents for access to their correctional files in the event of further research with their cases. Without hesitation, every woman gave written consent to an examination of case files, an unlikely attitude had anyone fabricated an account. To some degree, the request to follow up with later research acted to support their credibility. In addition, many participants struggled with painful emotions as they revisited abuse by male partners, the homicide event, the adjudication process, and their incarceration. Finally, through an unexpected chain of events, I was able to conduct an informal interview with the incarcerated daughter of a study participant—incarcerated for the same homicide—who described from her own perspective the same violent events told to me earlier by her estranged mother. Thus, an independent source corroborated this one woman's story.

Chapter Five

❧

A Profile of Convicted Survivors

*A Comparison of Battered Women Inmates
and California's Women Prisoners*

The United States of America incarcerates its citizens at alarmingly high rates. In 2000, the U.S. rate of incarceration (690 per 100,000) surpassed that of Russia (675 per 100,000), making it the world leader in imprisoning its citizens (The Sentencing Project 2001). The U.S. incarceration rate is at an all time high (The Sentencing Project 1999),[1] about six times the rate of Canada, ten times the rate of Sweden, and eighteen times the rate of Japan (The Sentencing Project 1997). Further, the U.S. surpassed other nations in the percent of change during the decade between 1985 and 1995 (The Sentencing Project 1997). While incarceration rates have increased for both men and women, since 1980 the rate of increase for women (almost 400 percent) is roughly double that for men (Morash, Bynum, and Koons 1998; Human Rights Watch 1996). Profiles of women inmates suggest that their crimes have not gotten more serious; rather the system is more willing to lock them away for increasingly longer periods of time. As rates of women's incarceration increase, the proportion of violent offenses shows a parallel decrease—one-third of all women prisoners serve sentences for non-violent drug offenses (Bloom, Chesney-Lind, and Owen 1994). As of midyear 2000, 92,688 women were in state or federal prisons (Beck and Karberg 2001).

With 160,655 inmates, California has the largest prison population in the U.S. (California Department of Corrections [CDC] 2001) and the second highest rate of growth in number of prisoners since 1983 (Clear and Cole 1997). In an unprecedented building boom, California opened three new prisons for women between 1987

57

and 1995 (California Department of Corrections [CDC] 2000). Currie (1998) observes,

> In California, the prison population has jumped sevenfold in less than two decades, and a shoplifter with two previous convictions for burglary can be sent to prison for life. (3)

California has the largest number of incarcerated women, as well as the world's largest women's prisons (Human Rights Watch 1996): the Central California Women's Facility (opened 1990) and its newer sister institution, Valley State Prison for Women (opened 1995), both located outside Chowchilla (Human Rights Watch 1996); together, these two prisons house nearly seven thousand women (CDC 2000).

Bloom's (1996) study of California women prisoners provides a representative profile of the state's female inmate population, a profile that corresponds with data from national surveys of women imprisoned in the United States (Snell 1994). In general, California women prisoners are very low income, disproportionately African American and Hispanic, undereducated, unskilled with sporadic employment histories and mostly young, single, heads of households, with the majority having at least two children (Bloom 1996). In 2000, California's female prisoner population hit a record high of 11,432 women (Beck and Karberg 2001). It is not known how many women are behind bars for killing abusive partners.

Who are the women who participated in the present research and what are their characteristics? Are there differences between imprisoned women who have killed their partners in order to survive and other women prisoners? Using data drawn from questionnaires administered to a nonrandom sample of women incarcerated at a California prison for the death of their male abusers, this chapter compares key characteristics of Bloom's statewide sample with participants in the present study. While the sample for this study is not randomly selected, responses from the current forty-two women provide sufficient information to generate a comparison of the two populations.

This study utilizes an abbreviated form of Bloom's (1996) survey instrument that generated her profile of California's women prisoners. Drawing from the same inmate population and asking many of the same questions supports the reliability of the ensuing demographic portraits and comparisons. Thus, a particular strength of this research is the direct comparison it makes between a generalizable sample of women prisoners and a subgroup of battered women inmates from within the same state—California. Questionnaire responses reveal marked differences between battered women who kill and the general population of California women prisoners. The following tables reflect the distinctiveness of women who are incarcerated for using lethal force to survive severe intimate violence.

Demographics

Women convicted for using lethal violence against their abusive partners differ from the broader population of California women prisoners on key demographic markers (Table 2), such as age, race and ethnicity, education, marital status, and means of support.

AGE

Battered women prisoners are older than other female inmates in California. The median age of women in the current study is 47 years, 14 years above the state sample of 33 years. One-half of the women in the homicide group are between 45 and 54 years of age while nearly half the general population of women inmates in California are between 25 and 34 years of age. Nearly two-thirds of the battered women are ages 45 or older. About 60 percent of California's women inmates are ages 34 or younger in contrast to less than 15 percent in the homicide group. Compared to Bloom's sample, six times more women in the current study are 55 years and older.

RACE

As with the age variable, racial composition of the two groups shows significant disparity. The present sample is predominantly white, 67 percent, in contrast to Bloom's 36 percent. African Americans represent close to one-half of all women inmates, but only 17 percent of the subsample under examination. Latinas comprise 14 percent of California's women prisoners but only 7 percent of the present group. The category, "other" makes up about 4 percent of the state inmates, about half that of the convicted survivor group, which includes two Native American and one Asian/Pacific Islander. Whether the racial composition of the current sample reflects the overall population of battered women homicide offenders at this prison is unknown. White women may be more likely to participate in the prison support group from which the sample is drawn.

Table 2
Comparing Characteristics of California Inmates
and Spousal Homicide Offenders

Characteristic	Bloom (1996) n = 294 (%)	Leonard (1997) n = 42 (%)
Age at interview		
18–24	11.2	4.8
25–34	48.2	9.5
35–44	27.9	21.4
45–54	10.5	50.0
55 and older	2.2	14.3
[Median age	33 years	47 years]
Race/Ethnicity		
White	36.0	67.0
Black	46.0	17.0
Hispanic	14.0	7.0
Other	4.0	7.0[a]
Education		
8th grade or less	7.4	2.4
Some high school	28.2	14.3[b]
High school graduate	14.6	7.1
Technical school	12.2	11.9
Some college or more	13.5	64.3[c]
Marital Status (at time of offense)		
Married	16.0	52.0[c]
Widowed	4.1	0
Divorced	23.1	17.0
Separated	12.2	11.9
Never Married	42.9	11.9
Pre-Arrest Employment		
Employed	46.3	52.4
Unemployed	53.7	47.7
Worked at legitimate job	37.1	52.4
Supported by others	9.2	35.7[e]
Public assistance	21.8	4.8
Drug dealing/sales	15.6	4.8
Illegal sources	12.3	0
Prostitution	3.7	0

[a]Other: Native American = 5%; Asian/Pacific Islander = 20.
[b]Includes 11.6% with GED (Bloom); and 4.8% with GED (Leonard).
[c]BA/BS 2.4%; graduate degree 2.4%.
[d]Includes common-law marriages.
[e]35.7% supported by spouse or partner.

EDUCATION

Convicted survivors are more educated than the average woman prisoner in California. Prior to incarceration, women in the homicide group achieved significantly higher levels of education than those in Bloom's research. Three-fourths of the spousal homicide offenders have training or education beyond high school, approximately three times more than the general population of women inmates. Twice as many women in the California sample quit school without graduating (35.6 percent versus 16.7 percent). Participants in the current research attained a high school diploma or higher at double the rate of other prisoners, 83.5 percent compared to 40.3 percent.

MARITAL STATUS

Women who cause the death of their abusive partners are much more likely to have been married than the average California female prisoner. About 43 percent of the state's women prisoners report that they have never been married and 20 percent are married or divorced. At the time of the homicide, more than half the current study participants were married, about 30 percent were divorced or separated, and only 12 percent had never been married.

EMPLOYMENT

At first glance, only a minor employment difference appears between the spousal homicide offenders and other women prisoners. Nearly equal proportions of both groups report being employed, full or part-time, prior to their arrest—Bloom: 46.3 percent; Leonard: 52.4 percent. However, closer examination reveals disparity in sources of financial support. The vast majority of women with spousal homicide cases (close to 90 percent) were either self-supporting or supported by a spouse or partner, compared to less than one-half (46.3 percent) the general population. Convicted survivors were nearly four times more likely to be supported by others—9.2 percent compared to 35.7 percent. Current study participants received public assistance at one-quarter the rate of other women prisoners, less than 5 percent versus nearly 22 percent. Drug dealing/sales, prostitution, or other illegal sources provided income for over six times as many women in Bloom's group, 31.6 percent compared to less than 5 percent of the homicide group. Among the formerly battered women, the most frequently cited reason for not working was the opposition of their husbands or boyfriends. The California cases point to problems with substance abuse as the main reason for not being employed.

In sum, women serving prison sentences for using lethal measures against their male abusers differ from their sister inmates on a number of key demographic variables. Measured against other female prisoners, convicted survivors are older, less likely to be women of color, and have attained higher levels of education. Women convicted for the death of abusive partners are much more likely than the general population of women inmates to have been married and supported by their partners.

Family Arrest History

Comparing the arrest histories of inmates' family members reveals further differences between convicted survivors and other women prisoners (Table 3). A greater proportion of women in the California sample report the arrest of family members than in the homicide group. Just over one-half of the present group relate a history of family arrest compared to more than two-thirds of Bloom's cases. Both groups report brothers as the relative most often arrested. Of particular interest for this research is the rate of arrests of spouses: husbands

Table 3
Family Member Arrest History

	Bloom (1996) n = 208 (%)	Leonard (1997) n = 42 (%)
Arrest		
Yes	71.0	52.4
No	29.0	47.6
Family Member		
Brother	58.0	23.8
Sister	29.0	4.8
Father	20.0	9.5
Mother	12.0	2.4
Husband	10.0	4.8
Son	7.0	2.4
Daughter	3.0	2.4
Other	14.0	2.4

Table 4
Substance Abuse Problem

	Bloom (1996) n = 294 (%)	Leonard (1997) n = 42 (%)
Substance		
Alcohol	28.0	26.0
Prescription drug	21.0	38.0
Illegal drug	24.0[2]	16.7

of battered women were half as likely to be arrested as husbands of other prisoners (4.8 percent versus 10 percent).

Substance Abuse

Reports of substance abuse shows both similarities and differences between the homicide group and Bloom's sample of California women prisoners (Table 4). Compared to convicted survivors, Bloom's women describe greater problem usage of illegal drugs but nearly identical rates of alcohol abuse (28 versus 26 percent). However, women in the current study report notably higher rates of prescription drug abuse—38 percent compared to 21 percent.

Physical, Emotional, and Sexual Abuse Histories

Women responded to numerous questions regarding past experiences of abuse, as children and as adults. Regardless of age and in all categories of abuse—physical, emotional, and sexual—women in the current study report dramatically higher rates of maltreatment and violence perpetrated against them (Table 5). There were no differences, however, in the most often named abusers across categories. As children, formerly battered women were twice as likely to experience physical abuse than women in the California sample. While the nature of the present study guarantees that 100 percent of the current respondents would report physical abuse in adulthood, more than half (59 percent) of Bloom's women acknowledge physical abuse in adult relationships. Women in the present investigation report nearly twice as much emotional abuse in childhood and more

Table 5
Child and Adult Abuse Histories

Type of abuse	Bloom (1996) n = 294 %	Leonard (1997) n = 42 %	Most named abuser
Physical abuse			
as a child	29.0	58.5	Father/stepfather/ mother
as an adult	59.0	100	Spouse/partner/ boyfriend
Emotional abuse			
as a child	40.0	76.0	Father/stepfather/ mother/stepmother
as an adult	48.0	98.0	Spouse/partner/ boyfriend
Sexual abuse			
as a child	31.0	54.8	Father/stepfather/ other male relative
as an adult	22.0	95.2	Spouse/partner boyfriend
Sexual assault			
as a child	17.0	47.6	Stranger/father/ step-father/family friend
as an adult	32.0	85.7	Spouse/partner boyfriend/stranger

than twice as much in adulthood than their California counterparts. As children, more than one-half (54.8 percent) the women in the homicide group experienced sexual abuse, compared to nearly one-third (31 percent) of the general population of women prisoners. Almost all women in the present study report sexual abuse as adults, while less than one-fourth of the women in Bloom's research experienced such abuse—95.2 percent versus 22 percent. As children, 17 percent of the California sample report sexual assault, a significantly lower rate than the 47.6 percent reported by the homicide group. Likewise, 85.7 percent of women in the current study report sexual assault as adults, while 32 percent of Bloom's women report adult sexual assault experiences.

Battered Women Inmates: Specific Characteristics

What are the legal outcomes for battered women homicide defendants? Of what specific crime have they been convicted and what sentences do they serve? Numerous researchers have documented the willingness of the criminal justice system to imprison women and to sentence them to long prison terms (Banister 1996; Bannister 1991; Bloom 1996; Chesney-Lind 1995; Ewing 1990; Mann 1992; McCorkel 1996; Osthoff 1991; Owen and Bloom 1995). The following data report the results of the trials and plea bargains of convicted survivors.

The majority of conviction offenses for female intimate homicide offenders fall into the more serious categories of homicide (Table 6). Out of forty-two women, only two were found guilty of voluntary manslaughter. Eighteen women were convicted of second-degree murder. First-degree murder is the most common conviction (52.4 percent) found in this sample.

An examination of sentencing patterns shows that the overwhelming majority of cases received lengthy and indeterminate prison sentences (Table 7). Only two women serve determinate

Table 6
Conviction Offense

Offense	(n = 42)	(%)
Voluntary manslaughter	2	5.0
Second degree murder	18	43.0[3]
First degree murder	22	52.4[4]

Table 7
Prison Sentences

Sentence length	(n = 42)	(%)
10 to 14 years	1	2.0
15 to 19 years	1	2.0
7 years to life	2	5.0
15 years to life	11	26.0
15+–20 to life	6	15.0
20+ –30 to life	14	34.0
30+ to life	1	2.0
Life without parole	6	15.0

sentences. Eighteen women serve sentences between seven and twenty years to life. (To date, both women serving terms of seven years to life have been in prison for approximately twenty-five years.) Fifteen women serve sentences exceeding twenty years to life and six received a sentence of life without the possibility of parole.

In the United States, research consistently shows that the variation among prison sentences for similar convictions can best be predicted by race. The present study shows marked differences by race, but not in the direction predicted by the criminological literature (Table 8). A sentence of seven years to life went to the Asian American/Pacific Islander interviewee. Both Native American participants received over fifteen years to twenty years to life. Sentencing of the four Hispanics ranges broadly from the determinate ten to fourteen years to life in prison without parole. Of the eight African Americans, courts sent one-half of the women to prison for fifteen years to life and the other half received more than twenty years to thirty years to life. One white woman was given a determinate sentence of fifteen to nineteen years, while the remaining received some form of life sentence. More than two-thirds of the white women serve sentences exceeding fifteen years to life and nearly all of the life without parole sentences went to white women. This sample shows an overrepresentation of whites among the longer sentences. Ninety percent (38 of 42) of the homicides are intraracial.

Legal counsel for the cases under examination include public, private, and a combination of public and private (Table 9). More than one-half the cases were handled by public defenders. Private

Table 8
Race and Length of Sentence

Sentence	Asian Am	African Am	Hispanic	Native Am	White
10 to 14 yr.			1		
15 to 19 yr.					1
7 yr. to life	1				1
15 yr. to life		4	1		6
15+–20 to life				2	4
20+–30 to life		4	1		9
30+ to life					1
Life w/o parole			1		5

Table 9
Legal Counsel

	(n = 42)	(%)
Representation by:		
Public Defender	23	55.0
Private Attorney	14	33.0
Private followed by Public	5	12.0

attorneys defended one-third of the women. After exhausting their resources, five women were forced to replace their private attorneys with public defenders. There appear to be no significant differences between those sentences received by women represented by public defenders and those represented by private attorneys.

Conclusion

This description of battered women who killed their abusers differs substantially on most points from that of the general population of women prisoners provided in Bloom's (1996) statewide profile, a profile that corresponds to national surveys. Compared to other female inmates, women in the homicide group are older, have more education beyond high school, and are unlikely to have been on public assistance. The majority of women in the homicide group under examination are white. It can be argued that this demographic group is more likely to seek out the help of a support group and thus may be less a representative reflection of all battered women homicide offenders. However, Bannister's (1996) examination of 275 similar cases drawn from the National Clearinghouse for the Defense of Battered Women reveals a similar contrast with the California and national profiles of women prisoners:

> More than sixty percent of the women in the Clearinghouse data are white. Approximately 30 percent are African American, and a small number are Latina, Native American, or Asian. These percentages are not representative of female homicide rates generally. Nationally, more nonwhite women are arrested for homicides than are white women. (82)

Family members of battered women who kill are less likely to have been arrested. Women in the current study who report substance abuse problems prior to incarceration are more likely to have abused prescription drugs and less likely to have abused illegal drugs, a pattern opposite to the state profile. In childhood and adulthood, women in the homicide group suffered significantly more physical, emotional, and sexual abuse. In addition, Bloom's research reveals that 40 percent of the general female population had been on probation or parole immediately prior to incarceration, while fewer than 20 percent of the present group had any previous arrest history. The most common prior arrest reported by the homicide group was for motor vehicle violations.

While the emerging portrait of convicted survivors contrasts with that of other California female inmates, it bears a close resemblance to Ewing's summary of several studies on battered women who kill and Browne's spousal homicide sample (see chapter 2). Ewing describes high rates of abuse—sexual, physical, and emotional—and the likelihood that the battered woman who kills is older. In her study of women who killed their abusers, Browne (1987) found that nearly three-fourths reported

> some kind of physical violence in their childhood homes, including that of a father or other male partner abusing their mother, abuse of siblings, abuse of themselves by parents, and abuse from other relatives. (23)

Just as women in the current study are virtually devoid of criminal histories, Browne (1987) notes that battered women who kill "have the least extensive criminal records of any female offenders" (11). However, women in the present group appear to have attained more education than those described in Ewing's summary.

Based on information reported by current study participants, prosecutors, judges, and juries show little sympathy or lenience toward battered women who kill their abusers. Despite a clear lack of criminal or violent histories, the overwhelming majority of these women are convicted of first or second degree murder and receive long, harsh sentences whether they are represented by private or by public attorneys. This finding suggests the possibility of a systematic criminal justice bias against battered women who kill. Moreover, California women prisoners see that parole boards rarely release women convicted of spousal homicide; thus, those with indeterminate sentences perceive their sentences to be the equivalent of life without parole. Indeed, life without the possibility of parole is not a rare prison term for convicted survivors.

Contrary to the bulk of criminological research, in the cases of battered women who kill, it seems that being white does not grant an advantage. While the current method of sampling precludes generalizing results to the overall population of battered women inmates, the figures reported here suggest that white women who are found guilty of killing their male partners do not occupy a position of privilege as they stand before the bench for sentencing. On the contrary, their social status seems to work against them. In her analysis of legal outcomes for women who killed their male intimates, Bannister (1996) concurs, "White women have a much greater chance of receiving a longer prison sentence than do non-white women" (85). Considering that the homicides in this study are most often intraracial, as is the case for the overwhelming majority of battered women who kill[5] (Bannister, 1996; Mann 1992), it can be argued that it is the victim's color or social status that determines the position of privilege in the criminal justice system. Similarly, Bannister (1996) observes, "Women who killed higher status victims more often were convicted and they received longer sentences" (86). Further, of the thirty-nine women on death row in 1992, "two-thirds of their victims were white and three-quarters were adult males (where these data are known)" (Streib 1992, 182). Women in the present study seem to be punished more harshly for killing a white male than for killing a man of color. Further, differential gender role expectations based on a woman's race or ethnicity may provide additional explanation—is it even more unacceptable when a white woman uses violence? Bannister raises the possibility that white women receive longer sentences because they are likely to resemble the wives of the trial judges, judges who may identify with the deceased male partners.

Part II

⌇

Narratives of Personal Experiences:
An Introduction

The convicted survivors of intimate violence who form the core of the present study describe and interpret their lives by narrating them. As they responded to open-ended interview questions, women produced narrative accounts of their personal experiences from childhood to incarceration. Although the women did not report every violent episode, nor go into great detail on every event that they did discuss, they provide a rich, textured glimpse into the personal and social realities of partner violence. The stories that follow reflect homicides that occurred between 1977 and 1994.

Allowing women their own voices is fundamental to the nature and purpose of this study. Rather than filtering women's language through the interpretive lens of another, this study uses the interviewees' own words, thereby reducing the potential for distortion and misrepresentation. Each convicted survivor is the expert on her own life. Only she can reconstruct her own life-world and expose its particular trajectory. Each individual woman presents a subjective standpoint that allows us insight to her thoughts, her perceived options, and her actions. The perspectives of these women are crucial if we seek to examine and learn from their experiences and their circumstances.

The life histories of incarcerated battered women demonstrate internal consistency and coherent life paths that make sense of their violent experiences. Constructing narratives allows the women to discover previously unseen connections among episodes, among relationships, and among the time periods of their lives. Each woman in the study tells a unique and deeply personal story. Yet, each story resembles the stories of other women interviewees. While the women's pre-prison lives vary by class, by culture, and by race, their abuse-related experiences and outcomes suggest few differences.

Through their narratives, women express common themes and describe common patterns. This research suggests that, where intimate violence occurs, gender overrides other social categories. The life accounts of convicted survivors need to be examined in relation to the private and public contexts in which they occur.

Chapter Six

∼

Minimizing and Forgetting Violence

"The backhand? I didn't consider it hitting, because it was above the neck."

Introduction

Almost without fail, responses from the women reflect a nonobvious theme: women continue to minimize or forget the violence they suffered at the hands of their abusers. Practitioners and researchers note that forgetting abuse experiences is common among survivors. Kelly (1990) observes, "We forget experiences in order to cope with an event that we do not understand, cannot name, or that places acute stress on our emotional resources" (124). Battered women frequently minimize the degree of violence in their relationships (Browne 1995). Despite a great deal of self-education, support group interaction, and reflection on the events that preceded their incarceration, former victims repeatedly minimize the significance and effect of the violence they experience.

Narratives

Because research shows that pregnancy provides little relief for a woman who has an abusive mate (Martin et al. 2001; McFarlane, Parker, Soeken, and Bullock 1992; Stark and Flitcraft 1988), each woman was asked if the abuse continued during her pregnancy. A forty-year-old mother of two answered no, that there had been no abuse during either of her two pregnancies. Later in the interview, she mentioned that he "backhanded" her on the head continuously throughout their marriage. Asked if the backhanding stopped during the pregnancies, she states,

> When I was pregnant, he didn't beat me. He was always the mental abuse and always the backhanding on my head; that's why I get a lot of headaches. He didn't hit me when I was pregnant. The backhand? I didn't consider it hitting, because it was above the neck. [with a laugh] Yes he did!

Frequently, a man who is physically abusive subjects his partner to sexual abuse as well. Regarding sexual abuse, the same respondent states:

> I don't know if there was sexual abuse. I don't know. It's like, there was a time when we were first in our marriage, I was pregnant, he had a girlfriend living with us and he wanted a ménage a trois kind of thing. Just to get him to leave me alone, go do what he needed to do. We'd been married not even a year, half a year, something like that. It was like, what he wanted, I got. I had no choice. It wasn't that . . . Even now when I talk about it, I leave. I have a lot of blank in my mind.

When this woman was asked about his attempts on her life, she responds:

> He didn't make any direct attempts on my life. He just needed to tell me.

However, later in the interview, she observes:

> I have no doubt that he could kill me. There was one time that he had me against the wall, my feet off the ground, I was going into convulsions and I scared him because he couldn't bring me out of it. That's the nicest he'd ever been, after that situation, because it scared him so bad. He came close to killing me, and then in bed when he'd wake up and he was in Vietnam. Yeah, I was seeing stars!

One woman states repeatedly that her husband never laid a hand on her, that the abuse had been limited to mental abuse.

He didn't *physically* abuse me, so at that time I didn't even know that domestic violence was the mental abuse. Of course it was just all *me*. So I was going to do what I had to, to keep the marriage together.

Later she recounts an episode that took place in the office of their hardware store, but, because it didn't fit into her own definition, she did not consider it physical abuse. After tearing up the office and throwing items at her for accidentally double-billing one of his friends,

He grabbed me by the throat, shoved me up against the wall; his friend had to pull him off of me.

However, when she describes the nonphysical, mental abuse, she recounts her husband's ongoing, ritualized threats to kill their two daughters and then to kill her:

The first night he did that, I thought it was all talk. But it became a nightly ritual. He'd get that gun, point it at me, and he'd go, "If you think I'm kidding . . ." and he'd take the gun and walk into the kids' room with the gun.

Another woman initially reports only

bruises. Cuts. Didn't have any broken bones. I never went to the hospital.

Later in the interview, she recalls:

Mostly there was slapping, slapping me, spitting on me, verbally abusing me, telling me I'm trash, the block whore, just belittling me, like nothing. Making me feel like I was all that . . . He was drinking a beer. He had hit me in the head with it . . . and there was blood squirting out of my head.

The following comes from a woman who later showed me several small scars on her face, head, and hands:

He'd get angry and—he wouldn't hit me with his *hands*—all through our marriage I didn't think that I was really being physically abused because he wouldn't hit me with his hands. He would throw things. They'd accidentally hit me. Beer bottles if he had one in his hand; a wrench if he was working on his car; a gun if he was planning on shooting me and decided he didn't want to so he'd throw it at me; he'd kick a door in on my head; he'd drive a car off the road if he was mad at me for some reason; throwing plates at me, dishes, a broom; whatever he happened to have in his hand. He'd punch a hole through—I'd just happen to be in front of a door or a window, whatever it was, he'd punch a hole through it and hit me. Glass and all.

One woman recalls a violent episode only after being reminded by her daughter who had witnessed the attack.

I want to think that my kids didn't know, but in reality, even my youngest, only three at the time, she remembers things. How do you remember that? She told me after I was out on bail, she said, "I remember when Daddy had the knife and he broke the mirror. He's not mad at you anymore." I say, "How do you remember that? What do you remember?" She said, "Daddy was mad and threw the mirror and the mirror broke, and he had a knife at your throat." I didn't even remember it. Until she brought it up, I didn't remember that incident.

Another woman describes memory gaps filled in by her children:

My attorney . . . talked mostly to my daughters. Most information he got, he got from them about the abuse, and incidents that had took place, because there were some that I didn't remember.

Even a former nurse with an extensive medical background minimizes the physical damage:

The only physical injuries—just concussions and stitches, that's all.

However, she later admits,

He tried to kill me two or three times that I'm sure of. He tried to drown me in the bathtub once. One of his biggest things was choking me. [weeping] I'm very lucky to be alive.

Conclusion

When a woman is held hostage in an abusive situation from which she sees no escape, minimizing or forgetting the violence serves as an effective denial mechanism that helps her survive (Graham, Rawlings, and Rimini 1990). Once she is no longer subject to ongoing violence, a woman may be able to recall and redefine particular events as violent and abusive. In the course of the interviews, several women were able to identify and re-label specific episodes and actions as abusive or violent. The process of redefinition allows women to shift the blame from themselves to the abuser, a crucial step in their recovery and growing self-empowerment.

Chapter Seven

~

Self-Identifying as a Battered Woman

"I never considered myself a battered woman."

Introduction

As the interview process unfolded, I became aware that, had I sought out these cases a few years earlier, many of the respondents would have excluded themselves from the study. Along with minimizing or forgetting the violence, only a few considered themselves battered or abused women during the violent relationship and in the early part of their incarceration. While interviewing women survivors of male violence, Fine (1995, 437) notes with irony that women who have been abused often distance themselves from precisely those labels (such as "battered woman") feminists use to heighten public recognition of the gendered nature of such violence. For many of the women in the present study, the first realization that they had been victims of domestic violence occurred as they began attending a support group for battered women in prison; and for some, the process took several years.

Narratives

One woman reported that the first eight years of her twenty-two-year marriage were free of violence. However, over the ensuing years, his outbursts of brutality left her with multiple injuries from physical and sexual assaults.

> I just didn't think of me as being a battered woman for about fifteen years. When they said that I could get help at battered

shelters and when I went to file a restraining order, she told me that if I had to I could go and take the kids to a shelter for battered women. I said, "No, I don't need that because I don't fit that." She didn't give give me any information then about battered women. I didn't get anything to read about battered women until I was in [this group].

A mother of three stated:

I never considered myself a battered woman. If someone had asked me then if I was a victim of domestic violence, I would have said no. Believe it or not, even during my trial, I still didn't think I was a battered woman. It wasn't that bad. Until I came to prison and joined CWAA and heard other people's stories, like, well, that's just like mine!

At fourteen years old, this woman's parents gave her to her husband, a man twice her age. Her comments reflect the link between her victimization in adulthood and in childhood.

If someone had asked me then if I was a battered woman, I'd have probably said no, or I don't know. Because I lived that way as a child and I believed that's the way it was supposed to be. I knew inside myself that something was wrong and I didn't feel good, but I didn't know *why* it didn't feel good. It hurt.

A mother of three suffered numerous injuries from ongoing physical, emotional, and sexual violence throughout her sixteen-year marriage.

I didn't even know what domestic abuse [or violence] was, much less what he was doing. I had no idea what [the terminology] meant. I was not allowed friends. I was not allowed phone calls. He would mark the tires or check the odometer on the car. He would mark the driveway, using soapstone, or whatever it was he used.

The next respondent experienced severe physical and sexual abuse, known by numerous outsiders, including law enforcement.

Nobody ever referred to me as a battered woman. "Battered woman" was never mentioned. If anybody had asked in a survey then if I was a battered woman . . . or a victim of domestic abuse, "No." I didn't feel I was a battered woman but, because I fought back and there were times maybe when I egged it on. I see it all clearer now. But, I wasn't going to lay down. It was the only thing that was left of me.

The following statement comes from the woman who earlier described being slapped, stalked, and bloodied:

I never knew I was a battered woman until I came to CWAA. I told [the group leader], "I was never battered." She sat down and had a long talk with me. It's like, wow! I never realized that I was battered. When I realized it I actually called my brother. I never knew. I would've never known had I been out there. It explained a lot of things.

The following comments reveal some of the reasons one woman had not considered herself "eligible" to be called a victim, and the slow process of acquiring a new definition of the situation:

My idea of myself changed through a lot of therapy, a lot of [support] group setting, a lot of different women—women that were not sexually promiscuous, that did live in the house with the two-point-two kids and the one-half dog. Betty Crocker still was told the same things I was. That she was fat, ugly, stupid, a slut, a tramp, a whore. I came to the realization that mine wasn't unique. I'd heard the word "abuse" before. I'd seen a talk show here or there. Just because I didn't cower in a corner . . . That didn't make me any less battered or any less bruised or any less wounded. Betty Crocker still got exactly the same that I did. She may not have fought back but the tension building was there the same. It was the same picture to each person. They were just painted with different strokes and it took a year or two of hearing other people's stories to know that my story really wasn't any different. I could identify myself as a battered woman within about a year. It took me another two years or so to quit saying, "If I would shut up, he wouldn't have." It took me *another* year after that before deep inside my gut within the whole being of me I knew not just intellectually, but in my heart of hearts, that regardless of what I said or what I did *he had no right to hit me*.

Or demean me. Or to make me feel less of a person than I
was or that I am.

For some, denial was not so much a lack of understanding about
what constitutes domestic violence, rather it was based on shame.

I didn't call myself a battered wife. I called him a wife beater.
I didn't know about domestic violence. If I knew about it, it
was just a newscast and it was gone. If someone had called
taking a survey and asked me if I was a victim of domestic
violence, I'd have said no. They would have to ask, "Does
your husband ever beat you?" Besides I wouldn't have told
them. I'd have hung up. I didn't want anyone to know. I was
ashamed.

For another, denial was based on fear.

If someone had asked me if I was a battered woman, I'd
have said NO. I would deny being a victim of domestic violence. Because if someone asked me, even on the phone, [he]
would find out. I don't know how he would find out, but I
was scared.

Conclusion

For battered women, defining the experience of intimate violence is
a complex process. Months and years may pass before a female victim of domestic abuse redefines events and actions as part of an ongoing pattern of oppression and intimidation. It may take even more
time before she defines herself as a battered woman. Feminist scholars suggest that the lack of names given to women's experiences renders those experiences invisible and silent (Kelly 1990). Giving a
name to her experience empowers a battered woman and validates
her thoughts, feelings, and actions. Du Bois (1983, 108) explains:

The power of naming is at least two-fold: naming defines
the quality and value of that which is named—and it also
denies reality and value to that which is never named,
never uttered. That which has no name, that for which we
have no words or concepts, is rendered mute and invisible:
powerless to inform or transform our consciousness or our

experience, our understanding, our vision; powerless to claim its own existence. . . . This has been the situation of women in our world.

As formerly battered women in prison join together in support group and in personal conversation, they tell of lives structured by abuse, they hear common histories, and they begin the process of shifting definitions and naming their experiences. What had once been a private, personal problem becomes a social ill shared by other women convicted of spousal homicide, and women outside prison walls who are trapped in a virtual domestic prison by abusive male partners.

Chapter Eight

∾

Police Involvement

CALLING 911

"By the time they left, they had me believing I had done something to him to cause it."

Introduction

Law enforcement officials act as the first line of help for battered women, and as such, they are the gatekeepers to systemic response by prosecutors, judges, and social workers. Just how much family violence police actually see is not known, principally because "many officers still fail to define and record such incidents as crimes" (Sherman 1992, 5) and often fail to file any report at all (Ferraro 1989). Further, officers routinely categorize domestic assaults as misdemeanors, rather than as felonies (Browne 1987). In a survey of three hundred women using a battered woman's shelter, Abel and Suh (1987) found that three out of four women called for police aid, with officers responding 95 percent of the time; however, despite six out of ten women asking that their batterers be arrested, the police arrested abusers at less than half that rate. Pagelow (1981) reports that of the women in her shelter sample who asked police officers to arrest batterers, the majority was refused. A team of researchers found that, even when departmental policies directed officers to arrest offenders, the police made no arrest in 82 percent of the cases (Ferraro 1989); further, while these officers were required to give victims information on available protective procedures and resources, in sixty-seven out of sixty-nine cases they failed to do so without being prompted by the researchers.

Increased public awareness of the prevalence and nature of domestic violence has revealed the need for improved criminal justice
interventions. As a result, substantial policy change and reform has
occurred over the last decade, such as the pro-arrest policies enacted
by most states (Hamby 1998). However, policies, as Sullivan (1997,
162) observes, "are only as effective as the officers who implement
them and many police are still leery of pro-arrest policies." Even
when perpetrators are arrested, they seldom go to jail; thus the batterers' pattern of coercion and control is reinforced and women's access to help is further blocked (Stark 1996). Correspondingly, a
National Institute of Justice review of civil orders of protection
found police failure in three areas: failure to inform victims of their
options, delay in serving the orders on offender, and failure to arrest
the abuser when he violates the order (Sherman 1992). In the majority of cases in the present study, women sought the help of law enforcement to stop their partners' violence. They reported the attacks
only to be left with even less hope and feeling more trapped.

Narratives

For this interviewee, law enforcement failed to meet her needs a
number of times, even up to the day of the homicide:

> I called the police many, many, many times. Nothing hap-
> pened. Sometimes they came out. If they came, they said he
> had a hard week at work, because he could change when
> they'd take him over there to talk. I was bleeding, my nose
> was bleeding. They wasn't going to arrest him. Well, he'd
> been choking me and, trying to get his hands down, I had
> scratched him. He said, "If you're going to arrest me, I want
> her arrested." *Then* they were willing to take us. But they
> wouldn't take him. They said, "You can go to your daughters,
> go to your friends." They'd been there so many times they
> knew my neighbor. How many times did I call? Hundreds.
> How many times did someone show up? Maybe half the
> times I called, they showed up. If it was women officers on,
> more. If it was men officers, they'd come an hour, two hours
> later. Maybe they took him four, three times. But, the boys
> [that he threatened with the rifle], that incident was differ-
> ent. He wasn't charged for me, they just put him in the
> drunk tank. [T]he police never said anything about getting

help. He'd just tried to shoot me earlier [on the day he died].
I called the police. "What do you want us to do, lady? It's his
house. We can't get him out."

In the next case, the woman's estranged daughter independently
corroborated the family's experiences with police unresponsiveness
when I interviewed her during an unrelated research project as she
served a sentence at a California Youth Authority facility for her
involvement in the same homicide. In the mother's words:

> The police, every time I called them, they were usually there
> about thirty minutes or so, but by the time they left, they had
> me believing *I* had done something to him to cause it. [When
> he tore up the tire shop, threatening to kill me and the kids],
> I went across the street and called them. They got there in
> about forty-five minutes. He was already acting like he was
> completely sober and had been all day . . . but when the cops
> got there, and [my teenage daughter] was trying to tell them
> that he has been threatening all of our lives, they told her to
> shut up, and if she didn't, he was going to take her in. She
> was just trying to let them know. Then they told me the shop
> was in his name . . . too. My name on there made no differ-
> ence. None. It was his and that if I didn't want to be taken to
> jail that I'd better get out of there and leave it to him.

She continues:

> Once we had to go to the Burger King because I couldn't stay
> at home, because he was there [even after starting the di-
> vorce]. We put all the cats, and the dogs, and our little pigs,
> in the back of the station wagon. We didn't think he'd do
> anything to the horses right then. We got all the other ani-
> mals in the car and went to Burger King and I called the po-
> lice from there. They got out there in about thirty minutes
> and I told them what went on. My kids were telling them
> too. The guy said that it was a domestic problem and I would
> have to find a shelter to go to, or somebody's house and stay
> with them until he cooled down. They wouldn't even go over
> to the house and make *him* leave. It was always me! It was
> my house. I paid the payments. I made the down payment on
> it. But I was always being told that I have to leave, or they'd
> take me to jail.

In the following example, officers heard the batterer's threats and witnessed his violence.

> There was a prison halfway house next door. They called the police more than once. He had broke out the bay window and the police heard him threatening to kill me. His hands were on my throat and his knee in my chest when they broke into the house and pulled him off me. He was not arrested. He was walked around the corner and taken to his parents' house.

One agitated husband solved the problem of police inaction:

> One time in particular, he beat me really bad in the face. He was arrested for that. He was always very cautious not to hit me too much in the face after that. I called the police. It was terrible. The police kept saying over and over there wasn't anything they could do. It was a domestic dispute and it was something we had to work out; they hadn't seen him do anything so therefore, they could not arrest him. "Lady, if you want to file charges, you can come down tomorrow and file charges, but you could have done that to yourself; anybody could have done it to you." And I'm crying and hysterical saying, "Shine the flashlight in my face. See what he did to my face." I had a bloody nose, puffed up lips. They would just persist in being totally indifferent. So we tried various ways, "You want him to leave? Okay, we'll wait here while *he* leaves." I'm going, "Yeah, and he can come right back!" Their solution was for me to leave. So okay, where am I supposed to go? It was real frustrating. He was getting kind of agitated again, I'm hysterical, and we've got like three or four police officers standing around. He ends up slugging me in the face in front of the police officers, putting his wrists out saying, "Handcuff me. Handcuff me and take me. She's not going to be happy until I go to jail." They arrested him. They charged him for hitting me *once*.

She goes on to describe her sense of futility and her children's involvement:

> I now know that my kids basically grew up calling the police. When things would get hairy and scary for them [weeping],

they would call the police. The way my children would describe it is, when something would start, they would at some point try to defend me. But when he got angry, his fists and hands and things would just be flying at anybody. So he would hit the kids, too, if they would try to step in and make him stop. He would just go like crazy and he'd get all over everybody. Early on, the kids just learned to run to the farthest phone and call the police. Sometimes the police came; sometimes they didn't. Usually on calls like that the police don't come right away . . . By the time the police would arrive, [he has] either somewhat stopped or cooled down somewhat. He had a real knack for being able to [snaps fingers] switch real fast when the police would knock at the door. He was the calm one—I was the hysterical one.

This mother paid the price for following police advice:

When he was violent with me, the police were called and they said they could not arrest him because they didn't see him hit me. One time I had to place him under citizen's arrest because he had hit me in the head with a bottle. He was drinking a beer. He had hit me in the head with it. The cops got out and stated, "We didn't see him do it so we can't arrest him. The only way we could take him is if you place him under citizen's arrest." I go, "Do you know what he's going to do with me?" They said that's the only way. So I did it. Wrong thing to do. He didn't even get down to the police station. They took him down to his mom's house and dropped him off. Then I really got the ass kicked in.

He continued to harass her throughout the period of estrangement.

He used to come up there in the middle of the night and break out my windows. I was constantly replacing windows. These window people knew me. I'd call the cops, and they'd say, "It's dark outside. How do you know he did it?" So I just stopped calling the cops. For what? They don't . . . You just get tired. You just get tired.

For a six foot four inch, 250-pound former policeman, his network of friends and former colleagues rendered him nearly arrest-proof. The man's well-placed connections placed his five foot two inch, eighty-pound estranged wife at greater risk and calls into question the objectivity of officers assigned to investigate the homicide.

> I'd keep calling the police, keep calling, keep calling, until they knew my whole first, middle, and last name, and everything about me . . . There was an outstanding warrant for his arrest at the time of his death. He had a copy of it that he showed me that day. He said, "What do you know about this warrant right here?" I said, "Nothing. I'm telling you the truth! I don't know anything about it." He goes, "No, you know I know better. I have friends. I can kill you that easily [snaps fingers] and nothing will ever happen to me." They claimed he was never arrested because they didn't know where was at. However, my husband had worked with them—the same officers that worked the domestic violence unit also worked robbery and homicide. So they all knew each other. I knew more than anything, the biggest reason why he was never picked up was that they just chose not to.

Conclusion

While the nature of the research sample greatly increases the likelihood of finding ineffective police response, without exception, study participants who called on law enforcement for help did not receive the assistance they needed desperately. In the cases under review, officers repeatedly trivialized or failed to perceive the seriousness of the situation and the danger to women and children posed by violent men. After attacking, terrorizing, and/or threatening their partners, batterers may take a ride in a police vehicle—not to the county jail in handcuffs but to a relative's home. If officers decide that the man may remain on the scene, it is the woman who must leave her home or business for temporary respite or recovery from injury. When that occurs, the man's right to maintain access to his property outweighs the woman's right to be free from assault. In the face of such indifference or hostility, traumatized women and children are left feeling abandoned, unimportant, and over time, they become disillusioned with the system they had looked to for help and for justice. In addition, children and family members witness the violence and the subsequent ineffectual police action, leaving some with the impression that officials minimize the situation, that there will be no help from outside sources, and that the only way for the battered woman to survive is for the batterer to die. Thus, interviewees list brothers, nephews, sons, and a daughter among their codefendants.

When police respond to domestic violence incidents, they bring with them a blend of personal histories, cultural beliefs, and departmental policies. In some of the present cases, it is possible that law enforcement officers felt constrained by departmental policies and the nature of the domestic violence statutes of the time. However, even when policies dictate arrest, research consistently reveals the tendency of many law enforcement agents to resist bringing the full force of the law to bear on batterers (Abel and Suh 1987; Buzawa and Buzawa 1996; Ferraro 1989; Pagelow 1981 and 1992; Sipe and Hall 1996). Pagelow (1992, 95) observes:

> [P]olice officers always consider the wife somewhat responsible, particularly when there is alleged antagonism by the woman and when the man threatens violence. The husband's threats to harm his wife *lower* his responsibility, and the wife's responsibility *increases* as his threats are repeated. (emphasis in original)

Women in the current study report their inability to get police to protect them. Their stories of failed attempts to obtain help from law enforcement personnel mirror the stories of many other women who ultimately bring about the death of their violent mates (Gillespie 1989).

BARRIERS TO CALLING 911

"I knew not to call the cops on him—because he would get out anyway."

Introduction

Not all victims of violence call on law enforcement for help. The Department of Justice reports that most intimate partner victimizations are not reported to police at all (Tjaden and Thoennes 2000). The Department of Justice finds that women do not report partner violence mainly because they (1) consider it a private or personal matter; (2) fear reprisal; (3) view the crime as minor or are unsure that the attack was a crime; (4) believe police will not bother, are biased, and/or are ineffective; (5) want to protect the offender (Rennison 2000). Interviewees describe diverse obstacles that interfered with their ability to enlist the aid of law enforcement for their abusive circumstances. Some were threatened directly and many lacked confidence in the effectiveness of calls to police.

Narratives

One mother of three explains her reasons for not calling for help from law enforcement:

> I never called the police. He was brought up in gangs. He got into trouble a lot. So he told me, "No one ever snitches on anyone." He would tell me some of the things that they would do to snitches in jail. I knew not to call the cops on him—because he would get out anyway.

From his past violence against her and against others, one woman took seriously the threats of her abuser.

> I never called the police . . . He told me if I ever told, he'd hurt me worse than I had ever been hurt in my whole life.

This respondent describes her one attempt to call for law enforcement aid. Her lack of confidence in police effectiveness is based on childhood experiences with a violent stepfather.

> I tried once to call nine-one-one. He came in when I was on the phone. He just walked up very calmly, picked the phone out of my hand, listened: "Our circuits are busy. Please hold. [laugh] An officer will be with you as soon as possible." It was on one of those recordings. He hung the phone up and told me very calmly, "Ever try that again, I'll kill you." That was the first and only time I tried. If the police would've come out there, taking my husband out and patting him on the back, giving the "good old boy" attitude and acting like one of the guys—laughing and talking about women, how they were all no good. I knew they weren't going to help me.

Her husband's social networks were obstacles faced by this interviewee, an upper-middle class mother of two.

> I never called the police. All his friends were judges, attorneys, police officers. His cousin was a sergeant at the police station that arrested me.

One woman, whose Marine husband was seventeen years her senior, faced a dual challenge: the isolation of living on a military base and her husband's military assignment. She did not call on law enforcement for rescue.

> Unfortunately he *was* the police. He was a military policeman. When everything started getting really bad we were living on base. It didn't help for me to call any of his [MP] friends because they took his side.

The next respondent affixes some of the blame for not calling police on her own deteriorating mental state.

> I never called the police on him. But for many years he made sure we didn't *have* a telephone. I didn't call the police because I was getting sick myself—the drinking, and my depression.

Because of the racism often found in American society, women of color face added problems in seeking help. The following woman's situation captures the problematic intersection of race, class, and gender. Rather than seek help, she felt responsible to maintain the reputation of her physician husband and her ethnic group.

> *No*, I never called the police. *No!* In a small town like that? Out of all the doctors, there was only two blacks. I didn't think I needed to call the white man and tell him about my husband's beating me and we going through this and that? *No!* We were already having a hard time sometime at the hospital because some patients would come in and they're drinking or something like that and they'd say, "I don't want no nigger doctor taking care of me." You know, that kind of thing. Coming from the South, you don't tell nobody—police, doctor—nothing like that about your husband, particularly a white man.

Conclusion

Women report numerous reasons for not calling the police. Some have such low expectations of law enforcement that the obvious risk entailed in calling 911 outweighs the perceived probability that officers will fail to respond effectively. Women fear the consequences of reporting—consequences sometimes graphically detailed by violent partners. Controlling a woman's access to a telephone is one of the isolation techniques used by some abusive mates, making it all the more unlikely that she can call for help. To a battered woman, her abuser's social or professional networks may appear to be insurmountable obstacles in the normal pathway to protection, as is the case when his friends or colleagues are the very ones charged with imposing legal sanctions (e.g., judges, police officers).

For some women, especially those who do not conform to racial stereotypes, racism compounds the difficulty in seeking outside intervention. As Rasche (1995) notes,

> Whether it's fear of police brutality against themselves and their men, or the fear of being viewed as a traitor for disclosing a problem which may tarnish the positive image the minority community has worked so hard to foster, these are problems with which white women simply do not have to contend. (258)

Chapter Nine

∼

Coercive Drugging

"I was a zombie."

Introduction

For the overwhelming majority of the battered women defendants in this study, the homicide arrest was their first experience with interrogation, arraignment, and/or commitment to a county jail facility. Frightened, confused, and often traumatized from a recent beating and their own lethal actions, women report that confinement in county jail was more trying than subsequent confinement in state prison. One recurrent criticism that arises from their jail time is the use of prescription drugs—antidepressants and mood-regulators—as ordered by jail medical staff. The use of psychotropic medication is common throughout most American correctional institutions and it has been criticized for its function as a form of institutional social control (Shaw 1982).

In comparing men's and women's penal institutions, McCorkel (1996, 171) finds that "women's institutions rely on the prescription of psychotropic drugs (e.g., tranquilizers) to restrict and control inmate behavior." Genders and Player (1987) report that British penal institutions administer antidepressants, sedatives, and tranquilizers five times more often to women than to men. In a study of women lifers, Jose (1985) observes,

> Psychotropic drugs are given to women who complain about depression or misbehave in the institution, in order to "help them" control their problems (and then these women are half asleep and walk around like patients in a mental hospital). (191)

95

According to Culliver, "The use of psychotropic drugs is 10 times higher in female prisons than in male prisons" (1993, 404). Even when medical and psychological conditions are taken into account, McCorkel (1996) reports that women prisoners are still at least twice as likely as men to be prescribed psychotropic drugs. One California woman prisoner began an advocacy group, Women Prisoners Convicted by Drugging, after being forced by jail staff to take a

> combination of Valium, Vistaril, Robaxin (a muscle relaxant), Elavil, Benadryl, Phenargan (a sedative), and Tylenol with codeine, dispensed four times daily. (Auerhahn and Leonard 2000, 606)

Chalke (1978) addresses the ethical problems facing prison psychiatrists in their use of chemical restraints on prisoners, raising the issue of drug treatment for the purpose of controlling individuals. Inmate-author Jack Henry Abbott (1981, 42–43) bases his condemnation of mood-altering medications in prison on his personal experiences with "institutional drugs:"

> They are *phenothiazine* drugs, and include Mellaril, Thorazine, Stelazine, Haldol. . . . These drugs, in this family, do not calm or sedate the nerves. They attack. . . . The drugs *turn* your nerves in upon yourself. Against your will, your resistance, your resolve are directed at your own tissues, your own muscles, reflexes, etc. These drugs are designed to render you so totally involved with yourself physically that all you can do is concentrate your entire being on holding yourself together. (Tying your shoes, for example.) You cannot cease trembling. . . . Those who need the drugs, who are ill, do *not* experience it the way we do. . . . [Y]ou are handed over to a "psychiatrist," who doesn't even look at you and who orders you placed on one of these drugs. (emphasis in original)

More than a decade later, based on his observations as a prison inmate, Hassine (1996, 79) offers this explanation for the generous use of psychotropic drugs:

> The reasoning seemed to be that every dose of medication taken by an inmate equaled one less fraction of a guard

needed to watch that inmate, and one less inmate who may pose a threat to anyone other than himself. Hence, overcrowding had brought about a merging of the psychiatric and corrections communities.

In addition to correctional institutions, nursing homes have come under scrutiny and criticism for their use of chemical restraints; recommendations have been made to move nursing homes and long-term care facilities toward a reduced or restraint-free environment (see Braun and Lipson 1993; U.S. Congress 1991).

Narratives

One woman's comments reveal the promise of psychological escape through drug treatment. She also exposes the trial advantage that comes to those who receive bail.

> When I was first arrested, they put me on drugs. They said I needed them—the doctor that was there. At that time, you want anything that will make you sleep. You don't want to think about what's happening. And everyone sleeps all day and all night. They do it by getting on to the drugs. I continued to stay on that drug (Mellaril? I don't remember what) and sleep. Luckily enough, I was bailed out so I fought my case on the street and I wasn't on drugs. I knew I had to testify.

In contrast, a woman who serves a seventeen to life sentence observes,

> Eleven months of being on Sinequan, and during the trial I took Mellaril four times a day. I fell asleep seven times during the trial.

This woman received a sentence of twenty-five plus four years to life:

> You're not comprehending, you're not real aware of what's going on. I'm not in la-la land but I was just mellow, you know, and I didn't know what was going on. I never realized what the seriousness was.

A former high school English teacher describes her self-presentation in the courtroom and the impact of drug treatment on her ability to testify. She serves a sentence of twenty-five years to life.

> The jail psychologist or psychiatrist put me on drugs in jail. I was too distraught to make a rational decision about medication. During the trial I was on both a tranquilizer and an antidepressant. I was not able to testify well—I was a zombie. They said I was cold and remorseless, not showing any emotion. I'm articulate—a college graduate with a graduate degree—the meds made me inarticulate.

A woman, twenty-four years into a sentence of seven years to life, describes the impact of the homicide and its aftermath in combination with "psych meds." Jail medications extensively blocked her awareness of events.

> In jail, the psych doctor decided to put me on drugs. I don't know what it was. I was in total shock. I did not even have a period for eight months. My whole body shut down—my mind, too. This was during the trial too. I don't remember coming to prison. I don't remember being sentenced. I don't remember going court . . . I was so knocked out, and tweaked out, and in shock that I could not tell you what the heck happened. I couldn't even begin to tell you. I don't even know if I testified.

Unable to recall the composition of the jury, one woman offers an explanation for the memory gap.

> I don't really remember the jury . . . They put me on psych meds about three months before the trial.

As a twenty-year-old with an addiction to illegal drugs at the time of the homicide, a woman exhibits concern over the combination of medications prescribed for her in jail.

> I don't know who decided I had to be on medications in jail. They gave me antidepressants and other drugs. I was on like four different types that should not have been mixed together. I didn't even know why I was getting it and I didn't want it.

Several interviewees expressed ambivalence toward the prescription of mood-altering medications. The first example also suggests questionable professional ethics on the part of the mental health professional who was involved in the case prior to and following the homicide.

> Deputies and a nurse ordered Vistaril and Phenergan. I was depressed and out of it so I did and didn't want it. I was taking shots in jail . . . and medications—antidepressants—that was ordered by somebody. I was hyperventilating. They called me the brown bag girl—they'd bring me little paper bags to breathe into while I was in jail. I begged to see a counselor and the same one that had seen me and my husband, [the man] who had told on me, told [my husband] what I had said to him in confidence, came to see me one time.

> The counselor or the jail nurse put me on Vistaril and Elavil. I was told to take them and I did. I wanted to and I didn't want to. They kept me on them during the trial. It lasted two months. I stopped the day I came to prison.

Others were unequivocal in their objection to medications given during their jail confinement.

> The doctor in jail prescribed Sinequan for me. I didn't want the drug. I only wanted something to get rid of the migraines and allow me to sleep at night. They gave it to me during the trial.

> The jail staff . . . decided I had to be on Mellaril, Lithium, Elavil, Sinequan, Vistaril. I didn't want to take it. I was on all of it during the trial.

> The doctors and attorneys decided I needed medications when I was in jail. They gave me psychotropic drugs that I didn't want. Even during the three months of the trial I was on Thorazine, Stelazine, Triavil, Desyrel, and others.

One respondent's daughter alerted her to the observable effects of the drug treatment. The woman defended her right to feel the emotions "normal" for her situation and she managed to exercise some control over her dosage.

At Sybil Brand [Los Angeles County Jail for women] they put me on Sinequan. When I was first arrested, they put me in a mental observation ward. They were giving me medication—a handful of pills. And I was taking the medication because a *doctor* was giving it to me so I must need it. Days went by and my daughter came to visit me and she was like, "Mom! What's wrong with you? What are they doing to you?" I knew I was sleepy all the time and I had trouble sorting things out. I asked the doctor, "What is this for and what is this for?" I started sneaking and not taking them all. But I asked him what they were for and they told me that they were antidepressants. I was furious because, to not be depressed in my situation would not be normal. I'm *supposed* to be depressed. When someone dies you go through the grieving. I just didn't just kill somebody. I killed somebody that I loved very much. I had the right to be depressed and I refused to take the medication.

A Native American woman repeatedly refused to take a psychotropic drug. She reports that jail staff attempted to coerce her into accepting the medication by withholding her mail. She took her complaint to a higher authority.

When I was in Sybil Brand, every day they were calling me to go upstairs to take Thorazine. I didn't want to be on that medication. I'd seen girls on that medication. And I wouldn't. I wouldn't. One time I went up to the court and I told the judge that they were holding my mail. They were trying to put me on these meds. I had two court orders where I was not allowed to go up there and be on meds—a court order—and for them to release my mail. Because they were telling me they were going to lock me up if I didn't take them. I said, "I'm not taking them." But it wasn't the judge ordering them, it was just Sybil Brand. I think it made a difference that I was a woman.

A minister's wife was given Sinequan from the day she asked for help for migraines until she left for state prison. When the verdict came in, she relates that observers noted,

I was so calm and cool and collected they could not believe it. Even the reporter told my family, "She is really taking this very well. I can't get over how calm she is." It was because of the medication I was on. It worked against me and my thinking capacity wasn't where it should have been.

Conclusion

The tendency of medical professionals to overprescribe mood-altering, psychotropic drugs for women is not exclusive to correctional institutions. Throughout the country, significantly more women than men receive prescriptions for tranquilizers and sedatives (Lott 1994). However, for a battered woman attempting to prepare a coherent legal defense in a homicide trial, the overuse of psychotropic drugs becomes even more problematic.

Throughout a woman's relationship with a batterer, he denies her the right to have a voice in her own life. Following the death of their abusers, accused women are arrested, jailed, and, not infrequently, ordered by jail staff to take tranquilizers and antidepressants. Some successfully refuse the medication. Some women are able to make bail and discontinue the drugs. In general, however, women accept the drug therapy, even when contrary to their wishes, because they are told they need it, because their batterers have forced compliance throughout the relationship, or because a drug-induced escape from reality may feel good in the short term. Regardless of the motivation, many interviewees report that psychotropic drugs directly interfered with their ability to participate in the preparation of their defense cases. When drugs inhibit clear thinking, accused women significantly are less able to make reasoned decisions, less able to contribute crucial information, and less able to follow the course of their own trials or plea bargains. Thus, the overuse of mood-altering drugs becomes a form of institutional victimization that continues the silencing of abused women and constitutes a violation of their right to present a self-defense.

Chapter Ten

~

Adjudication Processes

"The actual trial lasted three days. Picking a jury lasted two."

Introduction

When a battered woman uses deadly force against her abuser, a prosecutor has the option to not prosecute based on justification, or to indict her for criminal homicide. The law divides criminal homicide into two classes of offense, murder and manslaughter, each of which is further differentiated based on the person's state of mind at the time of the killing. In California, women who kill their abusive partners may be charged with first degree murder (e.g., premeditated, intentional killing), second degree murder (e.g., deliberate killing without premeditation), voluntary manslaughter (e.g., deliberate killing due to serious provocation or heat of passion), or involuntary manslaughter (e.g., killing resulting from recklessness or extreme negligence). The available legal defenses for battered women homicide offenders tend to be quite limited since most admit to the killing (Ewing 1987). Most women accused of killing their abusive male intimates are charged with first degree murder (Sipe and Hall 1996).

The following narratives demonstrate the difficulties and frustrations faced by women in the present study as prosecutors adjudicated their cases. Evidence of violent assaults against the women by their male intimates rarely entered the trial as evidence. Not infrequently, defense attorneys employed questionable strategies, demonstrated a lack of knowledge about the dynamics of abusive relationships, and/or seemed disinterested in the unfolding events. The reputations of abusive intimates were protected at the expense

103

of the battered women homicide defendants. Where available, I include information on the year and jurisdiction of the trials or plea bargains.

Narratives

Life without parole was the outcome for a woman who was thirty-four years of age when she killed her sexually and physically sadistic husband. During subsequent legal proceedings, she reports discovering that her attorney failed to contact people she felt would support her defense case.

> The public defender did his job. He defended the public—I wasn't the public. He had no experience with abuse issues. He hired a psychologist to come in. The first guy they had come in was a man, and I was really uncomfortable. I could not talk to a man. I'm like, "And what am I supposed to say to you?" He was a very nice man, but I couldn't talk to him. This was in LA County in 1988. My attorney was trying to go with the battered woman thing except he provided no expert testimony. Even the psychologist that he had was just in family practice. Once he tried to say anything about the battered women's syndrome, he asked, "So you have expert training in this field?" He said, "Well, no." They more or less told him to shut up. So [he] testified and made it sound like he got his license out of a Cracker Jack box.

At the age of twenty, a plea bargain netted a sentence of twenty-five years to life for a woman whose abuser killed her cat and tortured her sexually and physically. The Los Angeles County case took place in 1984 and provides further illustration of the gendered nature of intimate violence and its investigation.

> I couldn't talk to the lawyer or the police about the rapes and the sexual abuse because they were all males. Maybe if there had been a woman to talk to . . . At first they offered a manslaughter but my public defender said no. Then, later, he said he had a conflict and couldn't do my case. The other public defender said they offered me a twenty-five to life and, "If I take it to trial you'll get the death penalty because this is my first murder case."

The attorney in this case advised his client to turn down a plea bargain, which would have resulted in a much lower sentence than the final seventeen years to life she received. Her words also show how economic disadvantage translates into legal disadvantage.

> I had a public defender. I didn't know anything about being battered. Well, there was this one girl . . . in [jail] fighting a murder case and she goes, "Was he beating you up?" I go, "Yeah." She goes, "When you go back to court you ask them what about the battered woman's syndrome—or tell them about you being battered." When I went back in there, the attorney asked right in the courtroom. The DA goes, "You're not in here for being battered. You're in here for killing somebody." That was it. That was all. That was *all* that was ever said. No expert witness. No evaluation by a psychologist because I wouldn't pay him four hundred dollars. My attorney told me not to take the plea bargain because I would walk by the time the court was over. They offered me five years.

Although her brother killed her abusive husband, this woman serves life without parole for first degree murder and recollects her attorney's approach during a very speedy trial:

> He told me that I could never bring up anything about my abuse in the trial because it would give them a motive. I did not bring up anything about my abuse, my molestation. Nothing. He said they have to *prove* I'm guilty. They don't have to prove that I'm innocent. They don't have to prove my state of mind. The clincher is when they asked me how I felt when [he] died. I said I was relieved. Then I explained, not because he died but because I wouldn't be abused no more. That's about the extent of abuse I could get in because anything brought up about him was discarded because *he* wasn't on trial, I was. This was 1987 in LA County. I had a two-day trial.

Two teenagers, a daughter and a boy who lived with the family as a son, took extreme measures to ensure that the father would not follow through on his repeated threats to murder the family and their animals. When the woman and her daughter reported his threats, police officers told them that nothing could be done until the estranged husband acted on the threats. The interviewee, who knew of the teens' plans, accepted a plea bargain in 1992 in the hopes that the two youths would receive lighter sentences.

> In my trial I never had an advocate to come and talk to me. I never had a psychologist report, any of that stuff. I didn't go to trial. It was going on for about fifteen months and every time we had a court date, I'd have to go down to San Bernardino from the Riverside detention center. We'd get down there and they'd say it was postponed. Or [my attorney] wasn't there and twice he had some other lawyer sitting there for him because he couldn't be there. My lawyer *never ever* came to see me. One of his girls . . . would always come and talk to me. She's a paralegal. We went over the abuse, the threats. I don't know if it got in as evidence because he told me that if I didn't sign this plea bargain, [the kids] would probably get as much as I did—twenty-five to life for first degree murder—I didn't want to see them [weeping] in jail any longer than they had to. The only time I saw the lawyer was in the courtroom. When he came in for the plea bargain and they took us in this little room, he said that it would be the best thing for me to just sign the plea bargain.

Despite testimony from a male codefendant that she tried to prevent the killing of her abusive boyfriend, a young woman received a sentence of fifteen to life in a plea bargain. Revealing the power of family dynamics, she describes accepting the plea to spare her family the embarrassment of a public trial.

> I called my lawyer a thousand times a day. "What do you mean you can't get it down to some kind of assault or manslaughter charge?" He said they just wouldn't go for it. They just wanted me down. My mother wanted me down. She was scared because I started out with the death penalty. That was a huge thing hanging over my head. I told her I would kill myself because I would not let the state do it. I said I'll just kill myself. My mother freaked out and called the jail, so they came to get me—to talk to me. I said, "You guys don't understand. I couldn't even kill my brother [who terrorized and sexually assaulted her throughout her childhood], how am I going to kill *this* guy?" So, pretty much, my mother laid the Catholic guilt trip on me and I said okay. I sold my soul to the devil for fifteen to life. I didn't stand up

for myself. My family is very secretive and well-known in the community. "What are the neighbors going to think?" It was very embarrassing. They wouldn't let me have a trial.

After thirteen months of competent counsel, one woman's attorney was killed in a car accident. The public defender failed to meet the same standard or to utilize the information. She serves a sentence of twenty-nine years to life.

My first attorney had fifteen witnesses to stand up for me, law officers, doctors, and everything. But when I finally went to trial, the public defender that they had given me, he kept putting me off. He was just too tied up in death penalty cases and stuff that . . . he didn't present a case at all for me. He didn't call anybody for me. And at that point, I'd given up. Do whatever you want to do. I'm not going to do anything anyways. I'm not going to win anyway. The trial began about six months [after my first attorney's death]. And I'd seen my [new] attorney probably three times between that. I kept calling his office telling him to come over. He'd come over and he would talk to me about other cases. He never talked to me about my case. Never! And my investigator kept telling me, "You have to get you another attorney." "Oh, no. Oh, no." I didn't want to hurt his feelings. Ohhh!! I think, how stupid!

Although most intimate killings occur between same-race partners, racism triggered a homicide when a twenty-two-year-old Latina told her abusive Korean boyfriend that she was pregnant and that she planned to have their baby. He attacked her with the intent to force the miscarriage of what he considered a "two-headed monster" mixed-race baby. Her 1993 trial occurred in Long Beach.

I had a psychologist testify for me. I had neighbors testify for me, a nine-one-one call [from an earlier assault]. Even the witnesses for the prosecution were made to admit, yes, they saw him slap and hit me numerous times. They also testified that he said he didn't want the baby to be born, and he struck me before I shot him. Yet, I was still found guilty on second-degree murder and I'm doing fifteen to life plus four years for the gun. When the trial was so obviously going in my favor, the DA brought in photos and letters that had nothing to do with the trial but were allowed in to simply "dirty me up," which it did.

When one mother of two daughters made an attempt to discuss divorce, her husband began a nightly ritual of holding a gun to her head, threatening to kill her and the children. Her defense attorney's questionable strategy may have contributed to the life without parole sentence she received in 1984. A male codefendant was employed at their store.

> My trial was going so great—bailiffs and everyone, "Oh, you're walking. No problem." Then all of a sudden, my attorney—the only time he ever really talked to me—he said, "You're going on the stand. Tomorrow." He came to [the LA county jail] with five minutes left. "What am I going to say? What are you going to say?" "Oh you're an intelligent woman. You'll be able to answer all the questions." So when I came to court that morning, he said, "I want you to admit to your love affair." I said, "Why? Nobody knew anything about it. My family doesn't even know. That will devastate my family! That's saying I had something to do with it." "That's the way we have to go because if they hear that you're honest about all this, they'll believe you and you're going to walk. It's your only chance." I got up on the stand, admitted to having a love affair . . . They didn't basically have a thing on me, so if I I didn't take the stand I wouldn't be here today. *None* of my husband's threats came in. They put my youngest daughter on the stand because she was supposed to verify the fact that the time they claimed the murder happened that I was at school picking them up. That was basically the only evidence for me. They never put my psychologist, my gynecologist on. He said, "Well, if they decide on a death penalty, we'll use them during the penalty phase." That was all I had. When I tried saying my husband mentally abused me and I was afraid of him, all that was thrown out because *he* wasn't on trial and he wasn't here to defend the allegations I was making—*I* was on trial for murder, not for his abuse. So that was that. But during the penalty phase my attorney got a lot of people to testify on my behalf and afterwards, one of the jurors said that if she would have heard that during the trial she would have never found me guilty.

One woman, eighteen years of age when she married her forty-six-year-old husband, experienced his violence for the first time on their wedding night. She reports that her case was thrown out twice due to "illegal police actions" before her conviction and sentence of twenty-five years to life.

> The actual trial lasted three days. Picking a jury lasted two. This was in Pasadena in 1985. We weren't allowed to use anything negative against him. My attorney's defense was, we weren't trying to get out of the fact that I had committed a crime. I told him all along I didn't want that because I did commit the crime. I was guilty of a crime. I wasn't guilty of first or second degree. I told him, "I'm guilty of involuntary manslaughter. I'll settle for voluntary manslaughter even. Anything less than that and I'll fight." He kept trying to understand that my state of mind—I didn't know what was happening; something had clicked and I wasn't there. They wouldn't allow us to use temporary insanity or diminished capacity. He kept trying to figure out ways to convince the jury that this was an accident. There wasn't any expert witness; I did have a psychological exam but the DA lost it. It was taped and they were getting ready to transcribe it, and [the DA] came in and took it. So [my attorney] had nothing. They took everything, notes and everything. He was not called to testify. On my side, my brother, my aunt, and myself testified. We couldn't say about the threats. Every time we tried to get anything in, it was dismissed, because [my husband] was the victim. And he was dead. The only thing that got into the trial record about his abuse was that, if he was mad at somebody, he wouldn't talk for a long period of time—take it out on me. Nobody testified about the abuse.

At fourteen years old, a woman's parents sold her to a family acquaintance twice her age because "they were tired of contributing" to her support. Despite numerous calls to police about her husband's violence against her and their children, and despite his stays in a mental hospital, she received a sentence of twenty-five years to life in a 1982 Yuba County plea bargain.

> They overlooked all the abuse. His record of the police taking him and going to the mental hospital was never brought up. Nothing. I kept telling [my attorney] about the abuse. I kept

telling him about the cops coming out to the house and he says, "Well, I could subpoena those records but for every record I could subpoena, for everybody that you tell me that I can call, they'll just have somebody else to say it. I don't think we can do anything here. The only hope I can see for you is either the death penalty or life without parole unless you take a plea bargain."

At the time of the homicide, one woman had an airline ticket to another state in order to escape her husband's abuse and had made plans to move in with one of her adult children. In the 1991 Los Angeles County trial, her psychologist did not testify nor did her medical doctor give evidence regarding her history of abuse. The private attorney argued that the shooting was accidental. She serves a sentence of nineteen years to life.

My lawyer did not want me to say anything real harsh about the victim, because you got to remember the victim is dead. You can't paint the picture so bad that the jury . . . will, "Hmm, what is this? The poor victim isn't here anymore." I have scars on my face; he let me point that out, if I remember right. I had to have breast surgery—he'd hit me. The sexual abuse—he didn't let me tell a lot of. Then he got sick, and he went to the hospital in the middle of the trial. He came back and he asked for a new trial. He wasn't well. And the judge said NO. [The jury was] out for about a week. They didn't call the doctor that did the surgery on my [ruptured] appendix; they didn't call the mental health therapist. They got their subpoenas but they didn't get called. We got my attorney on 'ineffective counsel' and he wrote a declaration to the fact I was not represented to the best of his ability. He was not knowledgeable in battered woman's syndrome. He didn't feel it was a fair trial.

An expert witness offered testimony on battered women and one woman's daughters testified about their father's violence. This prisoner was tried twice in Kern County—a 1987 trial ended with a deadlocked jury and a 1988 trial resulted in a sentence of fifteen years to life.

There was an expert witness. While I was out on bail we probably did about fifteen hours or so where we talked. She

did a report—used her in trial. She testified that I was a battered woman. She presented her test findings, interview
findings, statistics. I thought myself that it was very effective. My daughters testified to the abuse. I testified. The
first judge would not allow molestation or the sexual mis-
conduct by my husband. He wouldn't allow my interrogation
[by] the detectives. Before they actually completed my book-
ing and everything, they were interviewing me. I was very
straightforward and basically talked about abuse, made
statements to the fact that I never thought I'd get out of
there alive, that he'd rip my head off, that I thought he was
going to kill me. I repeated it throughout. I went to trial
twice and both times the district attorney fought to keep
that record out. We fought to get it introduced to the jury. In
both cases, the judge always ruled that the jury could not
know about my interrogation, couldn't know what it con-
tained. I was acquitted of first degree murder. The jury they
hadn't voted on second degree. He told them they had to go
back and decide on the following charges. They were out a
few days and came back and said they were deadlocked.
They could not reach a decision. He called a mistrial. I had to
go through being arraigned again. A year later, I was tried
for second and found guilty. I couldn't believe it. I was dev-
astated. In the first trial, there were a few of the DA's witnesses that really helped my case. It really turned and was
favorable to me. Of course, he made sure he didn't use those
in the second trial.

The first jury deadlocked on a charge of manslaughter in the case of
one woman who, during the interview, displayed police photographs
of her swollen, bruised, and gashed body taken at the time of her arrest in 1986. Despite an expert witness and abundant evidence of
her boyfriend's violent assaults, she serves a sentence of seventeen
years to life. She believes that the jury found her guilty because of
her unconventional lifestyle.

My first trial I had eight innocent, four guilty of manslaughter. I had an alcoholic female attorney that was really push-
ing the battered woman syndrome. We were on the third or
fourth day of our side when she failed to show up. She went
on a drunk. But she had been drinking right along. I had an
expert witness. The moral behavior in the first trial didn't

have anything to *do* with the price of tea in China. They hadn't even brought a lot of the abuse in and she hadn't even gone to his psychiatrist yet. But, she was bringing it in. She was going on the battered woman's thing and that was even supporting of the manslaughter as it stood right then. Then she disappeared. I got another court-appointed attorney. The second trial we moved from San Diego to El Cajon. That judge let *every*thing come in. They brought in everything I had ever done. The women that had been involved in our lives. Everything. I still didn't even believe that was enough for the jury to find me guilty. It was pretty obvious we weren't having tea. They came back with second degree and I was just shocked. But they had made me sound so bad and by this time, after eleven months of being on [psych meds] I fell asleep seven times during the trial. My lawyer—I hadn't spent a lot of time with him. I didn't feel this man thought very highly of me. He had pretty much made me feel like a scumbag, and when I read my trial transcripts he called me "pond scum." My own attorney. They brought in [my boyfriend's] psychiatric reports in the second trial. He had told the psychiatrist why he was there, because he had been beating me up and he just couldn't seem to stop. He'd stabbed me, and that he saw plain white figures on the side of the road that told him what to do to me. *The man had audio and visual hallucinations.* That right there—I could have been screwing somebody in front of them and I would think that that would cut me loose.

The following example from a 1991 trial in Norwalk reveals one judge's attitude toward the battered woman syndrome. In addition, while ample medical and law enforcement records of this woman's ongoing severe abuse existed, very little of the documentation entered her trial.

In the trial, I brought that in about the abuse. The judge that I went before did not believe in battered woman syndrome. He said, "Battered woman syndrome shmendrome." He told me at the very end of my trial that he felt like I was battered far worse and for a longer period of time by [my husband] than [by my boyfriend who died] and that I didn't kill [my husband]. The expert witness that we had explained battered woman syndrome and the flashbacks and cycles.

When [the DA] asked me about flashbacks, I had to explain flashbacks and to bring up my [broken] jaw. I clicked my jaw in the courtroom. I went to act as if I was eating an apple, and [opens her jaw and produces very loud cracks, pops] that's a very loud and distinctive noise. They were just, oohh! I made the sound in the trial and I brought up different incidents that had happened with [him]. Neighbors testified as to things that they had seen. My daughter came to testify. The medical records were there but the only medical records that were actually entered as evidence were the statements from the emergency room where I had signed that I didn't want to prosecute. They were entered by [the DA]. And he put them before me and he said, "Is that your signature? You signed that you did not want to prosecute against this man but you supposedly say this man—you just had twenty-eight stitches in your ear, had your ear sewn back on, but you're saying you don't want to prosecute. Why would you not want to prosecute if somebody hurt you like that?" "I was afraid." I was afraid.

The battered woman syndrome can be a two-edged sword, as demonstrated in the following case of a woman with a well-documented history of violent victimization:

I was on the stand for four days. It was very frustrating. Everything that I said, I was a *liar*. They said I was a liar, and that I had premeditated it. They decided that they would go ahead and stipulate to the fact, everyone would agree to the fact that I was a battered woman. But, then that meant that that was the *motive*. That's why I killed him— because he abused me. I couldn't use it to defend me, but they could use it to prosecute me.

Conclusion

Women who have been attacked and terrorized by male partners find it difficult or impossible to discuss the painful, traumatic, and humiliating details of intimate assault with male police officers, male attorneys, and male psychologists. While female victims are well aware of the gendered character of physical and sexual battering, lawyers and investigators fail to adjust their approach to better

fit the experiences of these women. As a result, potentially exculpatory information is not investigated, crucial evidence remains undis-
covered, and women are left without an effective defense. In some
cases, a prosecutorial attack on the personal character of a woman
defendant or her irrelevant, past behavior overwhelms even ample
evidence of abuse.

Some accused women accept plea bargains to protect their children, to spare their families the humiliation of a trial, to avoid the
death penalty threatened by prosecutors, or to speed up what they
see as the inevitable, negative outcome. Others refuse plea bargains
because they are confident in the fairness of the system, because
they are ready to fight for themselves, because they feel they have
nothing to lose, or because they follow the instructions of their attorneys.

Despite the common etiology of domestic violence and spousal
homicide (Mercy and Saltzman 1989), criminal justice representatives routinely decontextualize the homicide event. Systematically,
attorneys and judges disconnect the woman's lethal action from the
batterer's ongoing, escalating violence and threats. The strategy of
prosecutors and the decisions of judges prevent study participants
from presenting their full stories and deny them the opportunity to
offer evidence in support their claims of self-defense. All too often,
defense attorneys neglect questions about abuse and fail to seek out
witnesses and/or documentation to support women's accounts of
abuse. Therefore, the trial proceedings depicted in this study consistently produce incomplete, distorted, or confusing pictures of events
for jury members.

Just as the lack of financial resources keeps some women
trapped in abusive relationships, the economic disadvantage of some
participants prevents the use of experienced, qualified expert witnesses in their trials. For women in the present study whose resources allowed them the use of domestic violence experts, judicial
constraints, prosecutorial strategies, and jury bias outweigh the influence of these informed opinions, and in some cases, an undisputed
record of victimization as well. Further, while defense expert witnesses participate more often in later trials due to procedural and
legislative changes, they often do so with mixed results and with
somewhat inconsistent credibility.

Chapter Eleven

~

Conclusion and Policy Implications

Interviews with imprisoned women offer us unique insights into the lives of women convicted for the deaths of abusive men. Their articulate narratives convey fear, fatigue, frustration, and resignation. Their collective voice describes a series of events and interactions that produces in each woman a firm belief that the unavoidable conclusion to the violent relationship is death—hers, his, or both, and perhaps other family members as well. The women whose experiences are featured in this research represent the tragic failure of numerous social systems to address violence against women by present and former husbands, lovers, and boyfriends.

In the beginning, women believe in and call upon diverse social systems—systems that, in the end, fail them and their children. Leading up to the homicide event, women undertake numerous tactics, trying to end the violence. Strategies that study participants used in their attempts to escape abuse include: seek the help of family and/or friends; seek counseling from mental health and/or religious practitioners; move out of the home; leave or try to leave the state; hide from the abuser; move his possessions out of the home; consult an attorney; attempt to move into a shelter for battered women; call law enforcement; report abuse to medical professionals; file for legal separation or divorce; get a divorce; obtain a restraining order; press charges, and ask that the man be arrested. These proactive survival strategies reveal the women to have been creative, persistent, and courageous. Unfortunately, their resistance strategies and escape attempts were met with indifference, disbelief, obstruction, and in some cases, active hostility by those from whom aid was needed. Repeatedly, battered women encounter a pattern of gender insensitivity and gender bias in the responses of authorities and institutions. What can be done to reduce the likelihood that other women will experience the same pattern of abuse and the same

115

pathway to prison? While the past three decades have seen improvements in services for victims of domestic violence, findings from this research point to the need for further changes in public policies and attitudes that act upon private lives.

Gender

The gender-specific nature of violence against female partners calls for policies and approaches that demonstrate awareness and responsiveness to gender dynamics. UNICEF (2000), recommends strategies and interventions that address the "gender dynamics of power, culture and economics" (13). Thus, more women need to be involved at all levels of the criminal justice process. In an attempt to make law enforcement resources more accessible to women, several countries have instituted either all-woman police stations with multidisciplinary female teams (e.g., Brazil, Argentina, Colombia, Costa Rica, Peru, Uruguay, and Venezuela) or stations with female civilian workers attached (e.g., Malaysia, Spain, Pakistan, and India) who have been trained to respond to the special needs of victim-survivors (UNICEF 2000).

Whether a case is one of domestic assault or homicide, battered women are better able to describe their experiences and explain their actions to female investigators, especially when it involves sexual abuse or torture. Many women in the present study found it much too painful to discuss humiliating and traumatic details of sexual maltreatment with male officers, male lawyers, male prosecutors, or male psychiatrists and psychologists, even if men displayed sensitivity and understanding to their plight. Frequently, women perceive that male authorities direct their sympathies toward abusive men rather than to the female victims. Interviewees feel that, in most cases, men who ask them questions do not believe them, are insensitive to the women's emotional and physical injuries, and blame women for men's violence. While study participants and their children lived in terror of violent men, they found it nearly impossible to convey to male agents of the criminal justice system the depth of their fear and intimidation.

RECOMMENDATIONS

Ongoing gender-sensitive, domestic violence education is indicated for all representatives of the criminal justice system. All jurisdictions need specially trained units of officers, counselor-advocates, and prosecutors to handle domestic violence cases. These units should be generously staffed with female professionals. Further, the unique dynamics of intimate violence require male and female personnel who are emotionally suited to the assignment.

Arrest and Prosecution

Mandatory arrest policies continue to generate debate among researchers and practitioners. Critics argue that mandatory arrest policies are inconsistent deterrents to future violence (Schmidt and Sherman 1998) and lead to backlash arrests of women who fight back, even verbally, against their male partners (Ferraro 1997). Supporters point out that mandatory arrest policies as part of a broader strategy of intervention—not as a singular response—reduce the overall rates of domestic violence by deterring recidivism and communicating societal condemnation of battering (Stark 1996). The systematic arrest of batterers is a critical symbol of society's opposition to the abuse of women. Further, how child witnesses of domestic violence define the experience is likely to be influenced by the extent and content of the criminal justice response, which, in turn, may effect the cycle of abuse, or "intergenerational transmission of violence" (Kantor and Jasinski 1998). Moreover, mandatory arrest policies appear to reduce racial bias in violence-related arrests (Randall 1991).

Interestingly, domestic violence appears to be the only violent crime for which arrest is applied so begrudgingly. Yet, the higher the social and legal price batterers are forced to pay, the greater the likelihood of a cessation or reduction of violence among chronic and sporadic abusers (Ellis and DeKeseredy 1997). Most victimizations by intimate partners are not reported to the police because victims believe the police would not or could not do anything on their behalf (Tjaden and Thoennes 2000). The assault on women by male partners must be viewed as a crime, not simply a "domestic" or personal problem. Even in jurisdictions where policy states that batterers are to be arrested, most men "are never arrested or prosecuted, and certainly not convicted" (Karmen 1995, 189). As this study illustrates, proactive institutionalized procedures are crucial in light of women's chronic minimization of the violence of intimates and the likelihood of increasing severity and frequency of abuse.

RECOMMENDATIONS

Law enforcement should arrest all abusers not acting in self-defense. Prosecution of batterers must proceed whether or not the victims press charges or cooperate with law enforcement. When implemented by well-trained personnel in a coordinated effort, mandatory arrest, aggressive prosecution, and increased penalties for batterers grant women greater freedom from abuse and retaliation while holding abusers accountable for their behavior. Additionally, such policies may contribute to lowering rates of intergenerational transmission of violence.

Medical Reporting

Domestic violence is a critical health problem as well as a serious crime of violence. Besides direct injury, women often suffer extensive health, emotional, and social consequences (Bell et al. 1996). Tjaden and Thoennes (2000, v) report, "the number of medical personnel treating injuries annually is in the millions." However, despite the increased attention given to the issue, many primary care clinicians still grossly underestimate the prevalence of domestic violence, fail to ask about domestic violence when examining injured patients, and fail to attend educational programs on domestic violence (Sugg et al. 1999). Moreover, the vast majority of domestic abuse victims, like the convicted survivors of this study, minimize the violence they have endured. Many continue to minimize the danger even when that violence becomes severe and life threatening. The vast majority of domestic abuse victims, like the convicted survivors of this study, are not likely to self-identify as battered women.

Until women are free from fear and coercive control, until they gain understanding of the dynamics of abusive relationships, until they have time to place their private experiences in the context of gender-based violence, the responsibility for rescue cannot rest solely on their own shoulders. Protocols that assist medical practitioners to recognize, document, and report cases of domestic violence provide important legal evidence for the prosecution of batterers (Crowell and Burgess 1996) as well as for the defense of women who kill their abusers. Cases surveyed here follow the pattern of increasing severity and frequency of violence common to abusive relationships. Interviewees who sought medical care express their frustration with medical personnel who fail to intervene when the injured woman is unable to report or to specify the nature of the situation herself. Abusive partners maintain their power and control whether they stay in close proximity to their victims in a hospital emergency room or remain at a distance. Participants report their firm belief in the inevitability of subsequent abuse regardless of a woman's unwillingness to report and they express their unanimous preference for mandated reporting by medical personnel. Commenting on mandated reports of abuse in medical settings, one interviewee noted that, by law, "children get protected and the elderly get protected, so why shouldn't we get the same protection? Aren't we worth as much as them?" While reporting is mandatory in military health care settings, some bases take an intermediate approach by reporting suspected woman abuse to Family Assistance personnel, where it stays confidential as long as the abuser enters and completes batterer treatment (Campbell 1996).

RECOMMENDATIONS

Findings from this research support the implementation or continuation of mandated reporting of abuse in medical settings. To better serve the needs of the millions of American women affected by intimate violence, health care systems need to require ongoing education for all medical personnel; specific protocols must be in place to identify and treat the physical and emotional consequences of intimate partner violence; medical and nursing school curricula must include extensive training; all health care offices and institutions should have brochures and pamphlets readily available to the public as well as to their clients.

Resources

Batterers frequently prevent their female partners from gaining economic independence and limit or prevent a woman's access to family or shared funds. Women in the current study lacked sufficient resources to escape their abusive partners, leaving them without alternatives. Interviewees who sought help from shelters found that there was no room for them at the opportune moment. When the limited number of shelters (about 1,200 in the United States [Crowell and Burgess 1996]) do have space available, desperate women seeking to escape violence discover that the length of stay is seldom longer than ninety days (Hamby 1998). Indeed, domestic violence is a major cause of homelessness for women and children (U.S. Conference of Mayors 1998). Browne and Williams (1989) report a marked decline in female-perpetrated homicides as legal and extralegal resources become increasingly available. However, the current number of shelters is insufficient to match the level of domestic assault against women.

RECOMMENDATIONS

Clearly, more shelters with expanded resources need to be established with links to transitional housing and out-of state placement where indicated. State and federal public assistance programs must take into account the short-term and long-term needs of victims of domestic violence and facilitate economic autonomy for women and their children. States should help women who leave abusers to protect the confidentiality of their new addresses by granting substitute or false addresses for mail and all public purposes (e.g., Department of Motor Vehicles, voter registration). For example, California's secretary of state oversees Safe At Home, a program that aids fleeing battered women and children by providing a substitute mailing address and forwarding service in order to keep their whereabouts confidential. Enhanced job skills and job placement are essential for long-term solutions for women and their children. Faith communities need to provide material as well as spiritual support for domestic violence survivors in their midst and to shed long overdue light on the issue. Other household movers are encouraged to follow the fine example set by PeopleMovers, a San Diego, California-based furniture moving company that provides free assistance to women fleeing domestic violence.

Restraining Orders

Orders of protection increase a woman's sense of self-empowerment and control over her situation while documenting the abuse and her efforts to end it (Crowell and Burgess 1996). Tjaden and Thoennes (2000) note that many victims seek a restraining order as an act of desperation after experiencing extensive problems and these orders are routinely violated. For many abused women, including those in the present sample, obtaining a restraining order can be very difficult. All too often, filing fees, transportation problems, qualifying restrictions, and slow-moving and confusing bureaucratic procedures effectively block a victim's ability to get an order of protection. Departing from the norm, an innovative Los Angeles judge permits domestic violence victims to obtain restraining orders via fax and allows trained advocates to file petitions for restraining orders by fax (Pincus 1997).

However, restraining orders do little more than leave a paper trail when judges refuse to mete out serious penalties to men who refuse to obey them. The usefulness of civil protection orders has been seriously limited by widespread lack of enforcement (Finn and Colson 1990). Buzawa and Buzawa (1996) note that violation of restraining orders remains a misdemeanor in most states and suggest that "such crimes may be downplayed simply because they are crimes against women, historically a disfavored group" (86–87).

RECOMMENDATIONS

Procedures for obtaining orders of protection need to be simplified and standardized, fees lowered or waived, and accessibility facilitated. Any female who requests a restraining order against a current or former intimate should be given information on battering relationships, safety plans, and shelters along with referrals to counseling and legal services. Automatic arrest is the appropriate first response to any violation of a restraining order, followed by strict judicial sanctioning.

Homicide Prosecution

Research participants suffered extreme abuse at the hands of intimate partners, their efforts to enlist help proving futile. When a woman finds no legal way to stop life-threatening violence, she determines that the only option left is the death of the abuser or her own death. When interviewees use their own agency to put a final end to the violence, they are punished severely. However, the lethal actions of a battered woman can only be understood when placed within the context of her ongoing victimization and the lack of outside help. The trials and plea bargains featured in this study routinely excluded evidence and testimony of ongoing, severe violence and threats against accused women. The result is a picture devoid of self-defensive action. Within the criminal justice system, battered women who kill are grouped together with drive-by shooters and other dangerous criminal offenders (Castel 1990), although these women are highly unlikely to have any history of criminal or violent behavior (Browne 1987; Leonard 2000). This finding raises the question as to whether one isolated traumatic incident turns an individual into a dangerous criminal.

In the American criminal justice system, it is left to the prosecutor's discretion what charges, if any, are filed against an accused battered woman. When prosecutors opt to proceed with homicide charges, the self-defensive acts of women become criminalized. Research consistently reveals gender bias against women in the courtroom (Schafran 1990, Welling et al. 1990). Often juries never hear of the pattern of escalating violence as abusive men refuse to let their partners leave or end the relationship. As this research demonstrates, even when documentation of abuse exists, it rarely enters into court proceedings. Moreover, judges, juries, prosecutors, and sometimes defense attorneys disbelieve women who are certain that they took lethal action in defense of their own lives. Women are found guilty even when they sustain serious injuries in the incident that led to the homicide. Prosecutors and juries focus on the sexist question, "Why didn't the woman just leave?" When judges exclude evidence of past victimization and instruct juries in ways that give them little option but to convict, women become double victims, once again controlled and silenced, once again told that the violence they endured was insignificant.

RECOMMENDATIONS

When extensive abuse triggers lethal self-defense, prosecutors need to differentiate career criminals from these situational offenders who pose no danger to society. If the prosecutor is determined to move the case forward, manslaughter is the charge that best fits the battered woman's experience, rather than the all-too-common first and second degree murder indictments. Judges and prosecutors should be required to attend in-depth, continuing legal education programs on domestic violence as a follow-up to required law school courses focusing on the subject. Juries need to be better educated on the dynamics and consequences of ongoing abuse through the use of expert testimony and they need to hear all available exculpatory evidence and testimony. Jury instructions must allow jurors to consider the lethality of male violence. Further, battered women held responsible for the death of abusive partners should be exempt from the death penalty.

Legal Assistance

In the vast majority of cases, police officers arriving on the scene of a homicide committed by a battered woman find a traumatized and terrified individual who willingly cooperates with their investigation. Interviewees state repeatedly that they were confident that, once they told the authorities what happened, everything would be fine—police and prosecutors would understand that victims of extreme violence and death threats are left with no alternative but to kill in self-defense or die. Women believe that it will be evident to authorities that the homicide was justified and they will be able to stay with and comfort their children. Indeed, police had been on the scene responding to women's 911 calls earlier the same day in several of the present cases. Contrary to their expectations, women find that their accounts, given without legal counsel or protection, are used against them as authorities construct the official version of events in order to secure a successful prosecution (Bannister 1993). By the time a woman secures an attorney, it may be too late. Moreover, defense attorneys who represented women in the present study seldom demonstrated any understanding of the impact of ongoing, severe abuse on their clients. As this research shows, defense attorneys can carry with them the same gender biases as other criminal justice representatives. Many women seldom see their attorneys, are not informed about plea negotiations, and are allowed little or no input on their defense cases.

RECOMMENDATIONS

Defense attorneys should be required to meet continuing education requirements of domestic violence classes as a follow-up to required law school courses focusing on the subject. Female professional or lay advocates with knowledge and experience in domestic violence and spousal killing need to be assigned to each battered woman homicide case to help the traumatized woman negotiate the confusing and intimidating adversarial system of criminal justice. Advocates can assist women defendants to construct a complete history of abuse and explain the unfolding process of adjudication, serving legal as well as therapeutic objectives. A well-documented history of escalating domestic violence can reduce the charges or allow for charges to be dismissed. Helping the woman to understand and articulate her own actions reduces the shame and increases her ability to mount a defense. Further, advocates can contribute to the accused individual's understanding of her legal options and rights, such as being informed on plea negotiations and the right to refuse pharmaceutical treatment. An organization such as The National Clearinghouse for the Defense of Battered Women in Philadelphia, which provides crucial information and materials to advocates and to legal professionals who assist battered women defendants, should be made known to defense attorneys.

Alternatives to Jail

Women who cannot afford to meet the cost of bail are in a disadvantaged position. Awaiting trial in jail makes everything more difficult for the battered woman defendant. Children are placed either with her family, the family of the deceased batterer, or in foster care. Regardless of placement, as the adult most closely bonded to her children, a battered woman's concerns center around the well-being of her children with whom she will have extremely limited or no contact. A battered woman defendant with no history of criminal behavior is not a danger to the community, and poses little or no risk of flight. Alternatives to jail would greatly reduce costs of pretrial incarceration, create space for more dangerous defendants, and allow families to begin the healing process (Austin, Bloom, and Donahue 1992). In addition, this research reveals a troubling pattern: jailed battered women charged with homicide are often drugged, leaving them further disempowered and disadvantaged; the influence of psychotropic drugs seriously interferes with a woman's ability to reflect on the course of events and to participate in her own self-defense.

RECOMMENDATIONS

A battered woman defendant should be released on her own recognizance so that she can provide financially for herself and maintain her household throughout the adjudication process. Alternatively, she and her children could be housed in the secure and supportive environment of a battered woman's shelter to await trial where she and her children would receive counseling for the trauma they have suffered. The use of chemical restraints on battered women defendants is a serious human rights violation and must be halted.

Community-Based Corrections

The state of California spends millions of dollars each year to imprison women—convicted survivors—who are the least likely of felons to repeat their crimes. As inmates, women homicide offenders tend to be "model prisoners," complying with institutional rules and parole board mandates. This research highlights the differences between convicted survivors and the general inmate population, including the interviewees' lack of prior criminal history. These women do not pose a danger to the community, and have the potential to become productive members of society—as taxpaying workers, members of families, contributors to their communities, and as advocates for family violence victims. When the criminal justice system believes that women must remain under the control of the correctional system, the option exists for them to be sent to a range of community-based residential and nonresidential programs that have been developed for women offenders (Austin, Bloom, and Donahue 1992). Placing a woman in a supervised community setting or closely monitoring her in her own home would allow the convicted survivor to contribute to society while holding her legally responsible for her lethal actions. The loss of family leave visits for women in this study[1] deprives children of their mothers' and grandmothers' input, influence, nurturance, and closeness and is destructive to family relationships. Study participants feel strongly the desire to educate their children and grandchildren about domestic violence in the hopes of preventing the intergenerational transmission of violence.

RECOMMENDATIONS

This research supports placing convicted survivors in community-based programs that allow women to support themselves and allow mothers to live with their children. This move would save millions of correctional dollars as well as millions of social service dollars spent to address the needs of children with mothers in prison. Furthermore, it is crucial that California reinstate family leave visits so women can maintain viable family ties critical to their children, which will not occur in crowded visiting rooms.

Post-Trial Efforts

Battered women homicide defendants are treated harshly by the criminal justice system, more harshly than men who kill in self-defense, and more harshly than men who kill their female partners (Gillespie 1989; Stout and Brown 1995). The severe penalties meted out to women serve to reinforce patriarchal attitudes that remind women that their proper place is in the home where men are to hold a monopoly on power and control (Bannister 1991). Sexism in the criminal justice system dictates that women stay within their gender role expectations or face severe consequences, the same message communicated to women by their abusive mates. Following a battered woman's conviction, she enters another world of total control. In a sad irony, some interviewees state that they feel safer in prison than they did on the outside where they were controlled by their abusers.

Women's proscribed gender roles do not grant them the option of using violence against violence. How else can we explain the life sentences given to all but two participants in the current study? What other explanation can we offer for women with sentences of seven years to life who remain in prison after more than twenty-five years?

RECOMMENDATIONS

Inmate-led support groups of battered women in prison provide education, growth, advocacy, and self-esteem for members; thus, all women's penal institutions should permit and support such groups. Interaction between community domestic violence experts and advocates and battered women inmates would advance the interests and efficacy of both groups. In addition, outside support groups for battered women convicted of homicide are needed in order to seek their parole, resentencing, and clemency.

This study exposes the need to explore the possibility of retrials or early release for women imprisoned for killing their batterers. At a minimum, convicted survivors should be favorably viewed by parole boards and granted early release dates. The pervasive sexism reflected in the cultural double standard found throughout society and demonstrated in sentencing and parole practices must be exposed and dismantled.

Education

Research findings point to the importance of educational programs at all levels of instruction and in the community at large. Children of battered women witness and experience abuse in their homes (Wolak and Finkelhor 1998). Dating violence remains a hidden problem for millions of young people (Ferguson 1998; Makepeace 1999). Primary and secondary schools can challenge traditional gender ideologies, teaching students that unequal power based on gender is unacceptable, that women and men are equals, that women and their work are to be taken seriously, and that relationship violence will not be tolerated. Workplace violence is often a manifestation and extension of domestic violence (Stark and Flitcraft 1996), at high cost to business and industry from "low productivity, absenteeism, and staff turnover" (UNICEF 2000, 16). Thus, a few companies such as the Polaroid Corporation, Marshalls Inc., and Liz Claiborne Inc. conduct domestic violence awareness sessions for their employees.

RECOMMENDATIONS

Because social behavior and cultural roles are learned at an early age, gender-specific programs to target awareness of dating violence should begin in elementary schools and be reinforced in junior high, high school, and college. Adult women need to be educated about their legal rights and what resources are available to them if their partners become abusive. Public service announcements and billboards can raise awareness of the reality and frequency of battering. Domestic violence awareness and in-service sessions should be built into business and industry training programs and support should be provided for the victims.

Legal professionals involved in family court must be educated about the danger in which battered women and children are placed while fighting for child custody or being court-ordered to arrange visitation with violent men. Religious schools and seminaries must institutionalize training and education on family maltreatment and violence against women in their curricula to enlighten spiritual leaders and enable them to better assist and advise the victims who look to them for help.

Final Thoughts

In sum, the narratives of women in this study reveal the ineffectiveness of social institutions to stop violent men and to protect women. Women minimize the violence done to them and exhibit a reluctance to identify themselves as battered women. Women's own failed attempts at nonviolent self-rescue result in their firm belief that someone's death is inevitable, most likely their own. When the woman survives the final violent episode, she is charged with murder and prosecuted with vigor in a trial that disallows sufficient evidence of abuse to explain her action as self-defense. She is further hampered in her trial or plea bargaining when jail staff prescribes heavy and/or mixed doses of psychotropic medications.

It would be comforting to believe that our present heightened sensitivity to female victims of domestic violence as well as recent policy reforms, such as mandatory arrest and mandatory counseling for batterers, create a safer environment for battered women, with a more responsive system and sufficient resources for victims. However, even a cursory review of the news and the research literature convinces us otherwise. Battered women who kill in self-defense still receive long, harsh sentences, and currently incarcerated women have virtually given up hope of parole. Parole board hearings seem to reenact the criminal trials, overlooking or excluding from consideration the years of abuse suffered by the women.

The abuse inflicted upon women in this study by their violent partners falls at the far end of the continuum in terms of severity. However, the extreme physical, sexual, mental, and emotional abuse perpetrated against women interviewees reflects the experiences of the 1,000 to 4,000 women who die each year at the hands of men who say, "If I can't have you, nobody can." In a very real sense, the women in this study provide a voice for the many women who do not survive that final violent assault. We need to learn from their experiences in order to save lives and reduce the levels of violence and fear in our nation's homes. As Convicted Women Against Abuse founder Brenda Clubine observes,

> Women have got to get out of abusive relationships. We all need to understand that any violent relationship is potentially lethal.

Chapter Twelve

~

Portraits

A Woman's Experience—STALKING

She was an eighteen-year-old single mother and he was twenty-eight years her senior when their relationship began. She later learned he had been married twice before and she had been the oldest of his three brides. She now serves a sentence of twenty-five years to life for killing her husband.

The dating relationship was like the moon. It was great. Wonderful. I guess it was everybody's fantasy relationship. The guy comes to the house, picks you up, go to a nice restaurant. He brings you flowers all the time, calls you all the time, makes sure you got home okay. We dated a couple of months then we moved in together. Then it was about a year when we got married. Nothing changed in the relationship when I moved in with him, other than we didn't go out. Or if we did, we didn't go out as much. We were together all the time. The first time I experienced any abuse from him was on our wedding night. I didn't get to the bedroom on time. I walked into the bedroom and I got slapped. I went flying into the wall. He said, "You better learn what your wedding vows said. To love, honor, and obey. Learn it." I thought this couldn't be happening. This couldn't the same person. I do remember saying, "I'm stuck. My God, I'm stuck." The next day he told me that he was sorry he hit me but I shouldn't have made him do it.

I couldn't go to a rescuer—because he'd be killed. I knew. I knew Norman would find me. He's found me before. I'd always left him when my daughter was out of state, when I knew he couldn't get to her. That was always in the summer.

129

I would leave and not tell anyone I had left. And he always found me. He *always* found me. And I don't know how it happened, because I'd go someplace and be a prisoner in that place because I wouldn't go outside. I'd hide in the car, do something. I'd think I did it all right. The last time I made it all the way to Arizona. I was hiding in one of these little hotels along Route Sixty-Six, no phones in the hotel, no nothing. I was hoping he'd think I went on the main drags, not the tacky old ones. And he found me. He found me. I took the cottage in the back, didn't use my real name. He found me somehow; I never knew. But from that day, I lost it. I came around the building, and I froze. I'd just gone two buildings down to the grocery store, a little market. I came back and there he was, leaning against his car. I walked up to him and said, "How did you find me?" He said, "Never mind that." That's when he told me, "If you ever leave me again, I'll kill them all." He meant my family. I knew he was serious. He had all their addresses. He knew where to go and I knew he'd do it. If he was crazy enough to threaten it, he was crazy enough to do it. I knew he would. That was the last time I tried. I was just waiting for death. I was already dead emotionally. So I was just kind of praying that it wouldn't take as long to die physically as it did emotionally.

The police attitude toward me was "a piece of dirt." I was "the low-life bitch who shot her husband." That's exactly what was told and said.

A Woman's Experience—COERCIVE CONTROL

They met when she was twenty-four and he was twenty-seven. Dating was wonderful. After the wedding, things were not so wonderful. She now serves a sentence of life without the possibility of parole for spousal homicide.

Direct attempts on my life? Like when he held me down and choked me, left marks on me? Or I'd wake up in the middle of the night with a gun pointed at my head. Or him sticking a gun in my mouth and threatening to pull the trigger. Digging a hole on our property, telling me it was my grave, and that he wouldn't be guilty of murder because he wouldn't kill me before he put me in it. Threats against my

family. When I did manage to get the guts to leave him, I had
three dollars in my pocket. I went to the bus station and the
bus station wasn't open. I sat around outside the building,
waiting for the bus to come so I could go in and get a ticket to
wherever the money would take me. And the bus didn't
come. And it didn't come. And then I heard the truck. It was
my pickup. I heard the horn honk. He knew I was there. *He
knew I was there.* He always knew everything. He knew
what I was thinking. He always knew. He always knew what
I was going to do before I did it. He took me home and he
scared me because he wasn't screaming; he wasn't hollering;
he wasn't throwing; and he didn't hit me. I didn't understand
that. I understood him hitting me and screaming and
yelling. But I didn't understand the silence. We drove home
and we sat in the truck and I sat there waiting. I kept hoping he would hurry up and get out so I could get out. I was
not allowed to exit the truck unless he got out first. I had to
have permission to leave his presence or that was insulting
him; that was disrespecting him. I sat there waiting and
waiting. We must have sat there twenty minutes before he
ever uttered a word. Even outside the bus station he never
said anything to me; he just kept honking the horn until I finally came around, and he went like this with his finger for
me to come to him. He finally told me, "Next time, I will not
come after you." Very calmly, quietly. I thought to myself,
"He's going to admit that it's over." I said, "Can we get help?
You willing to try one more time, and if it doesn't work, you'll
let me go?" He said, "I never said I'd let you go." I was, "But
you said you wouldn't come after me again." He said, "Not
like this. You'll come back to me begging me on your hands
and knees for me to take you back." I looked at him and said,
"What *ever* makes you think that if I managed to get away
from you that I'd come back to you, let alone on my *hands
and knees?*" He turned to look at me and I saw . . . the evil.
And he told me, "Trust me, you'll beg me." He sat and described to me what he would do to my mother, my grandpar-
ents. He told me he would continue on with each member of
my family until I came to him, begging him to stop. I knew
that I would never get away. I believed he was capable of
doing what he said he was going to do. I believed it without
any doubts. He always did everything he said was going
to do to me. The sexual abuse got worse. He started using

foreign objects. He used a gun on me rectally—a loaded gun. I remember begging him to pull the trigger. So I wouldn't have to suffer anymore. He said that was too easy. Told me it was too easy.

A Woman's Experience—Injuries and Threats

She was sixteen and he was twenty-three, six-foot-three, with big green eyes, freckles, and big muscles. She saw a knight in shining armor. In 1977, after sixteen and one-half years of marriage, she was found guilty of murder and conspiracy to murder and sent to prison for seven years to life. A male friend received eleven-to-life and was released in 1986. Her son pulled the trigger, was tried as a juvenile at age fourteen years, and was released in 1984. She remains in prison.

I was not allowed friends. I was not allowed phone calls. He would mark the tires or mark the driveway, using soapstone, or whatever it was he used. He would check the odometer on the car. Through the winter months, depending on the weather, construction work stopped. So, for a while, in order to pay the mortgage on the house and the car payments and stuff, he'd go pimp me and I paid the bills. The kids couldn't even take PE numerous times, because of the marks and stuff on their bodies. The PE teacher came to court and testified where they had marks on their bodies.

He liked knives although he liked his fists better. He was good at throwing knives. I've had my back screwed up. I had to learn how to walk all over again. I spent eighteen months in a back brace. Mostly my face and upper body got it. I've had my face look like ground round many, many times. My nose's been broken twice. My face is plastic, except for my left cheekbone. My collarbone's been broke. I've had a fillet knife through my hand. He took a buck-knife and tried to do an abortion on me. He was cutting the "bastard" out of me. This was the wee hours of the morning. I took a towel, put it against my stomach with the pillow and drove myself to the doctor's home. The next thing I remember I was passed out on his doorstep. The doctor patched me up, fixed me, repaired me. The doctor I had, he tried. He called the cops, the OB/GYN doctor, 'cause my husband had torn me up inside several times, and my doctor literally sewed me back together, 'cause he was using these sex toys and God only knows what. So he hurt me inside real bad, and my doctor patched me up, fixed me, repaired me many, many times. But the cops were Masonic buddies. They'd say, "We can't do anything about it. We'll notate it, but we can't do anything about it. It's a family situation. Until she'll press charges and she'll do this and she'll do that." But how are you gonna press charges on a homicidal maniac, somebody who's out to kill you anyway? I mean, come on. I may have been dumb, but I wasn't stupid. The cops, when they did show up, talked to him and patted him on the back and said, "You know how these damn women are."

He said he'd take and kill the kids; he'd cut me off; if he couldn't have me, nobody could; if he didn't want me, no other son-of-a-bitch was going to. I was damaged goods. Who wanted me and three bastards? I was too dumb, too stupid, too fat, too ugly, too whatever, that nobody would have me anyway. I was too dumb to know how to do anything. He had to teach me how to cook, had to teach me how to fuck, excuse the language. I had zero self-esteem, zero schooling, zero education—not really, but I was convinced I was stupid. He said it, I bought it.

I have had guns pointed at my head, "beg for your life, bitch." A thirty-eight, snub-nose was cocked at my head, "beg for your life, bitch, cry, show me you feel it, show me you're scared of me, and then you're going to fuck me. Thank me for beating you. I'm teaching you a lesson." And I told him, "Well, do me a favor, take me out of *your* misery, pull the damn trigger." Numerous times we fought over the gun. I guess something almost equivalent to playing Russian roulette. And the gun was loaded. I tried suicide so often I couldn't even tell you where to start.

He proceeded to drink, beat the hell out of me, went and had sex with our twelve-year-old daughter, although, he definitely was not drunk. I went, got on the phone, called the cops, telling 'em, "Look this bastard is in the process of doing all kinds of weird shit and I'm tired of it and you guys are coming out here and doing something about it." While I was gone, our middle son came in the back door, went into the living room closet, got the twelve-gauge shotgun, brought it back and proceeded to pump eight holes in him. He had just got off of my daughter.

I've gone up for parole over a dozen times. It's like I am a pile of shit. You get talked to like you're an animal. They treat you like you're stupid. They treat you like you have no feelings, emotions, common sense, or anything else. You are everything that your husband told you, plus some. You're every kind of a tramp. You're a cold-blooded murderer. To hear them talking, I'm worse than Charlie Manson and the whole Family, the Hillside Strangler, and Son of Sam, all rolled into one. Afterwards, your guts are chewed up, you have nightmares, you have flashbacks, your insides are just in total turmoil. It takes you a month or longer to get anything, you know, back in normalcy without just spacing out. All kinds of horrid, horrid memories are back in your life.

A Woman's Experience—DRUGS

Her friends introduced them in the hopes that, to reciprocate for his interest in her, he would provide a steady flow of drugs for their parties. For him, drugs provided an effective tool of control.

What attracted me to the man I'm here for was the drugs. I had done drugs before but I wasn't a user. Well, he wanted to impress me. This guy was about thirty years older than me. He tried to correct me, show me all his silk shoes and jewelry all this stuff. He drove an Excalibur. He was those kind of people where they use you as an ornament. And I know that he wanted me for an ornament. Years ago, when he was like twenty-five or thirty, he made his first million dollars in numbers and in heroin. I didn't even know that. I never did heroin. I'm caught up in all this stuff I don't even know what I'm caught up in. And I couldn't believe it, when I found out when I was here that I came out of a Mafia situation alive. Nobody told me the kind of person that I'm mixed up in. I guess I was naive.

One time, I needed some help and I called him and he was so excited to come over there, he used the drugs to try to get me there and keep me there. I still wasn't serious, I didn't do it yet. Then maybe six months later I went back over there and he locked me in. That was it. Kept me there and I think I never did leave for about a week or so. He had a dead bolt lock. He would do coke with me. He would talk

about my family and my kids and about my family life and
my parents, you know. He'd tell me my parents made up stories. He'd say, "You're lying. You lying bitch. That don't happen. You're exaggerating." So, I'm thinking maybe my
mother never did tell me the story and all these things my
father taught me and raised me up with. He was reprogram-
ming me.

The violence started when I'd want to leave. He'd trick
me, then he would find something, he would make up something. Maybe I used a glass and didn't wash it right, or used
the wrong soap or something. He would look for something
and he would terrify me. I don't even really want to think
about it. In those days he'd make me believe that I did something. I actually thought, "I had to do something for somebody to act like this." What did I do wrong? I'm usually so
careful and I didn't remember doing something like this. So
sometimes in order to get him off my back, is just to say "I
did. I'm sorry" or whatever, you know. Then he hit me, then
he's sorry. Then he'd try to buy me things, but I didn't want
nothing, you know. He'd lock me in. There's the deadbolt
locks. So I might as well get high. I'm high and the idea of
being locked in didn't hurt as much. There was plenty of
drugs. Forcing me to have sex with other guys. The man still
would have been obsessed with me even without the drugs.
He wouldn't ever have really let me go.

I'd seen him violent with other people. Like one guy, he
really liked me, and he knew that. He knew that I really
liked him. *He* got wind of it. I don't know if he knew we ever
went out. So when I was over there getting high one day, he
asked my friend to come over there and he pistol whipped
him, made him get on his knees and drop his pants.

He busted my head open, I went to the hospital and they
wanted me to tell? I said the man would kill me dead! I will
not tell you nothing. After the time he busted my head open,
I had changed. I never went back over to his house. I'm in
AA/NA. I was wanting to work the steps and I was doing
stuff for myself. He saw that I was beating it so he came out
here to try to destroy everything that I'm trying to build for
myself. He would buy everybody, the whole city of Ontario.
He lived in Woodland Hills and I tried to get away from him.
I'm not going back out there. The last time he tried to kill
me. I'm not going out there. Three years of that. I'm out here

so he started coming out here trying to buy everybody. He had enough money. He had people watching me, telling my neighbors, "If you see her come outside call me. I'll give you a hundred dollars."

I'm getting ready to go to church one day and he calls and says he's coming out. If I'm not there, I'm going to be sorry, so I should stay. When he comes he brings all these drugs and all this money. He always has at least five thousand dollars. He brings like sixty-five grams of coke—says he came to help me. "Can't you see I'm trying to get myself together?" He's going to help me, give me some drugs so I can sell them so I can have some money. I don't wanna sell drugs. "Well, you know somebody, let them do it." He wanted me to sample it to make sure it was good. He knows if I take some I'm gonna be wanting some more. So, eventually I smoke some.

We go to these people's house and while we're over there, he thought I took his drugs. He tried to shoot me and made me strip and tried to shoot their dog. He was all tripped out. We stayed over there a day and a half. Later, when he was going through his pockets and stuff he found the drugs, the ones he made me strip for. He humiliated me. And I'm really destroyed. By then I knew he was ready to kill me now. He's telling me, "Don't think 'cause your brother is here I'm not going to kill you." I run in the house to tell my brother, "He's trying to kill me." My brother tells me I'm paranoid and I'm tripping. So now nobody's going to help me. I'm just going to be dead.

A Woman's Experience—RELIGION

She was attracted to her husband when she met him in church. He was polite, cordial, clean cut, and he was a minister. She felt that it would be different with him.

I didn't want anyone to know that I was going through what I was going through with him. Being a minister, one day he would get himself together. The mental abuse was all along. Then the violent abuse started really heavy. Prior to it was like a push here, and a shove here. But it got really violent, really, really intense. I was being put up in a room and accused of anything, whatever he was going through. I would get hit upside the head for no reason at all in his temper tantrum. I would get stomped. That was the beginning of it and it gradually got worse and worse. I hid it. I wore glasses to church—big glasses—and they hang low, and my hair was longer and I could fix my hair to where they couldn't see it. And when I would wear my glasses my face was covered pretty much. I was always protecting him, not looking out for me, but protecting him. But by [his death] it had gotten real bad because he was going with one of the girls in the church, although he denied it but it was evident.

I had written about wives being submissive to their husbands and that's another thing that I became. I was very, very submissive to him because I felt that if I did a lot, I wouldn't cause more problems. But it didn't help me at all. And I was always trying to be so understanding towards him and talk with him in a manner to whereas "I'm here, I'm here for you." I used to use scriptures to him, telling him that God said, "Love thy wife as thyself." He died for the church. I would say, "The way you talk to me and treat me around other people and the way that you jump on me is not loving me like yourself." And I would use scriptures at him and it would make him very angry, very, very angry cause it was the truth.

I really prayed a lot, fasted a lot, read the Bible a lot, cried a lot, you know, went through a lot. I think that made it even worse by him being a pastor and going through the things that I was going through because I didn't think that I should have to go through them, being in the ministry. But like I said, I was always protecting him. I didn't call the police when he would jump on me because we lived in a new development at the end of a cul-de-sac and I felt that if I had the police in front of our house it would be the end of the ministry. I felt we were just getting ourselves together—being a minister, knowing the Word of God, we're supposed to be getting stuff together. My situation I think is different from a lot of other battered women for the simple reason that there was Christianity involved and my head was, God will work it out. But it takes both of us—God and us. And it took all three of us and not just two of us.

I was very confused. I just couldn't understand why I was going through the things that I was going through when all I had ever been with him was a helpmate. And I had

picked him up so much, so many times. I was in his corner
and I just didn't know what to do. I called the minister that
was like his mentor several times trying to set up an ap-
pointment with him and finally, I was able to meet. I told
him what was going on, the things that he was doing; I told
him about his drug problem; I told him about the girlfriend;
I told him about everything. I told about the fighting—I told
him about how I would grab a knife to keep him from jump-
ing me, beating me up. That was sort of my shield to keep
from getting beat up real bad. I told him about everything,
hoping that, him being his mentor, he would sit him down
and talk to him and try to bring him to his senses. Later I
called him and I said, "You didn't believe me when I was
telling you about the things at our house." And he said, "Well
it wasn't that I didn't believe you, it was just that it was so
unbelievable that he would do something like that."

No one else knew until I tried to commit suicide. I took a
bottle of pills that the doctor gave me for migraines because
he was arguing with me and said some very volatile things
to me. I was just at the verge of a breakdown at this point
and I was tired and without thinking I just took the pills.
That's when my children found out that I had been going
through what I was going through. Because he actually
thought I was going to die, he called my children. I was in a
coma for about three days. When I attempted the suicide the
counselor asked if we was having marital problems and I
said "No."

A Woman's Experience—CHILDREN

Found guilty of second degree murder with a sentence of fifteen
years to life, she was separated from her husband of twenty-four
years at the time he died. Recent changes in state policy render this
mother and grandmother, her three adult daughters, and her grandchildren no longer eligible for the quarterly overnight prison visits
that helped sustain them.

There were times I planned to leave, tried to leave.
There were times that *he* left. There were times that *I* left.
There were times that we lived apart. Off and on, off and on,
off and on. There were periods of time that we lived apart for

a year or so. What brought us back together? Financial needs, him wanting to get back together, I wanting to get back together for the security or such. One time in particular, it was my middle daughter. She had gotten into some problems and she was in a placement home. Towards the end of her high school, she wanted to return home and that was during the time when we had lived apart for about a year. The people from the group home and the court system insisted that the family had to be intact—mother and father both had to be there.

A beating situation that would last the longest would be a situation where it would start in the morning and the children would be around, and I would be around. He would start in by hitting one of them or hitting me. Or being very forceful, very angry, and very sullen. You could tell that steam was just rising out of his ears and everything. He would just go into a rage and either he'd be tearing something up or hitting me or something. It could go on for hours, to maybe all day with him basically holding us hostage there. Nobody moves. Nobody eats. Nobody goes to the bathroom. You don't answer the door. Sometimes I would have to beg him, "Well, so-and-so has a date. The guy is going to be showing up soon." Or, "She's got to go to work. Please just let her get ready and go to work." I'd have to ask him permission to go to the bathroom. We basically would just be there all day in this emotional state with him glaring at you, sitting in the same position, not even wanting to move. I'd characterize it as him just holding us hostage till he vented everything he needed to vent. He'd made a lot of threats—suicide threats, and threats that he'd kill us all. Always it was, "The only solution is for both of us to die." It was his famous phrase. I took it literally. I knew that he was capable of trying to kill himself. And my fears were that he would take us *all* out. He would. There were times when he'd threaten me with a sledge hammer, tire iron, basically anything that was handy. There were times when I begged him not to kill me. But at work, he was professional. He had a college education.

A battered woman is a woman who feels like she has no power, that she's alone, and that it's a no-win situation. Someone else is always calling the shots and it's very difficult to ever see yourself out of that situation. There's no end.

You're trapped. Something I've noticed, there's a real difference between a person who's able to say, "Oh yeah, I had an abusive boyfriend, or I had an abusive husband. I divorced him and then I married this other guy and he was abusive so I divorced him." There's a big difference between someone who can't seem to get themselves out of that situation. I think that's where a lot of us run into the problem. It's terrible when you feel so trapped and the system's not there to help—everything's ineffective. You keep turning from one thing to another and you're just beside yourself. The realization is, it's never really over, it's never going to be over until *he* says it's going to be over. You don't have any say so. Because there are times when women have moved as far away as they can, and what does he do? He follows them. It's really particularly hard when you have children by that man. Because there's always going to be that tie there, and the court allows him to have that tie. I know people who have reported to the court, "You allow this man to come pick the child up and he beats me in front of the child as he takes the child away for visitation. Nothing's changed." Women are still scared and women still feel like they're the victim and they don't have an awful lot of chance because it's a man's world.

Appendix A

INFORMED CONSENT STATEMENT

My name is Elizabeth Leonard. I am a doctoral student in the Sociology program at the University of California, Riverside. I am interviewing women at CIW because I am interested in the experiences of women who are serving time for killing their abusive male partners. The purpose of my study is to learn what life was like for a woman in a battering relationship, what brings a woman to kill her abuser, what circumstances lead to conviction and imprisonment, and what her life is like in prison. Also, I am interested in learning about any contact with people or agencies like doctors, police, or counselors that may be related to the abuse.

Your participation in the project is completely voluntary and you may refuse to participate all together, or at any time during the interview process. *You are not required to answer any questions that you choose not to. All research information will be handled in the strictest confidence.* Your identity will not be disclosed in any reports or publications. If the interview is recorded, the tape will have a research number on it for identification purposes instead of your name. The tapes will remain in the sole possession of the researcher and will be kept for two years after the end of the study, then destroyed. *Maintaining the security of research records is of the highest priority.*

I UNDERSTAND THAT I AM VOLUNTEERING TO TAKE PART IN THE STUDY DESCRIBED ABOVE. I UNDERSTAND THAT I CAN END MY PARTICIPATION AT ANY TIME. I UNDERSTAND THAT I CAN REFUSE TO HAVE MY INTERVIEW TAPE RECORDED.

_____ Yes, I give my consent to be tape-recorded.

_____ No, I do not give my consent to be tape-recorded.

_____   _____
Printed Name of Respondent   CDC Number

_____   _____
Signature of Respondent   Date

INFORMED CONSENT STATEMENT

My name is Elizabeth Leonard. I am a doctoral student in the Sociology program at the University of California, Riverside. I am conducting research with women at CIW because I am interested in the experiences of women who are serving time for killing their abusive male partners. The purpose of my study is to learn what life was like for a woman in a battering relationship, what brings a woman to kill her abuser, what circumstances lead to conviction and imprisonment, and what her life is like in prison. Also, I am interested in learning about any contact with people or agencies like doctors, police, or counselors that may be related to the abuse.

In addition to interviews, my research may include the examination of CDC files of the women that I meet with. Your continuing participation in the project is completely voluntary. You are not required to allow me access to your case file. All research information will be handled in the strictest confidence. Your identity will not be disclosed in any reports or publications. Maintaining the security of research records is of the highest priority.

I UNDERSTAND THAT I AM VOLUNTEERING TO TAKE PART IN THE STUDY DESCRIBED ABOVE. I UNDERSTAND THAT I CAN END MY PARTICIPATION AT ANY TIME. I UNDERSTAND THAT I CAN REFUSE TO ALLOW THE RESEARCHER ACCESS TO MY CDC FILE.

_____ Yes, I will allow the above researcher access to my c-file.

_____ No, I do not allow the above researcher access to my c-file.

_____   _____
Printed Name of Respondent   CDC Number

_____   _____
Signature of Respondent   Date

Appendix B

QUESTIONNAIRE

I. PERSONAL INFORMATION

1. How do you describe your race and ethnic origin?

   _____ White, not Hispanic   _____ White, Hispanic
   _____ Black, not Hispanic   _____ Black, Hispanic
   _____ Native American   _____ Asian
   _____ Pacific Islander   _____ Mixed
   _____ Other

2. What was your age at your last birthday?   _____

3. What was your marital status right before the offense that sent you to prison?

   _____ Married   _____ Separated
   _____ Divorced   _____ Widowed
   _____ Single   _____ Common-law
   _____ Other _____

4. What is your religious preference?

   _____ Protestant   _____ Catholic
   _____ Muslim   _____ Buddhist
   _____ no preference   _____ agnostic/atheist
   _____ other _____

5. What is the highest level of school you have completed, including any vocational/   technical school?

   _____ less than Elementary   _____ Elementary school
   _____ 1–3 years HS, no GED   _____ 1–3 years HS & GED
   _____ 4 years of HS   _____ technical/voc. school
   _____ 1–3 years college   _____ 4 or more yrs. college
   _____ BA/BS   _____ graduate degree

6. Was this completed on the streets or in prison?
   _____ streets   _____ prison

7. For those with college: What was your primary subject in college?

_____

8. For those with voc/tech school: What did you study?

_____

Did you complete the course? _____ Yes _____ No

9. How did you support yourself (and family) before prison?

_____ primary source of income
_____ secondary source of income

Codes:
   1. working at a legitimate job/business
   2. spouse or partner
   3. family or friends
   4. AFDC, SSI or other public assistance
   5. unemployment compensation
   6. other (legal) _____
   7. drug dealing/sales
   8. prostitution
   9. shoplifting, fencing, etc.
   10. other (illegal) _____

10. Was this family income enough to support you and your family?
    _____ Yes _____ No

11. For those not working: What were your reasons?

    _____ _____ _____

    Codes:
    1. was looking for work
    2. no jobs available
    3. spouse/family supported me
    4. did not have training/education
    5. child care responsibilities
    6. transportation problems
    7. was in school/training
    8. drug/alcohol problem
    9. ill/handicap

10. had more w/public aid
11. more $ w/illegal acts
12. other _____
99. was working

12. What kinds of jobs have you ever had?   _____

_____

_____ no job ever

13. What is the highest annual salary you earned from working?

_____

FAMILY HISTORY

14. Have any members of your family ever been arrested?
    _____ Yes   _____ No

15. Have any members of your family ever been in jail/prison?
    _____ Yes   _____ No

    If yes:
16. Who?   _____   _____   _____

    Codes:

1. mother	6. step-sister	11. other relative
2. father	7. husband	12. other guardian
3. sister	8. son	13. none at all
4. brother	9. daughter	14. other
5. step-brother	10. boyfriend	99. N/A

    If any parent/guardian incarcerated:
17. Was this while growing up/in their care?
    _____ Yes   _____ No   Who? _____

ARREST AND SENTENCE INFORMATION

18. How many times have you been arrested as an adult?   _____

19. How old were you the first time you were arrested?   _____

20. What offense were you arrested for the first time?

    _____

21. Is this your only arrest? _____ Yes _____ No

22. What offense(s) were you convicted of that resulted in this in
    this prison term? _____ _____ _____

    Codes:
    1. homicide   4. assault
    2. voluntary manslaughter   5. weapons offense
    3. involuntary manslaughter   6. conspiracy (+ #1)
    7. other _____

23. Do you have codefendants? _____ Yes—male
    _____ Yes—female _____ No (If no, ⇒ Q#26)

    If yes:
24. Is/are they serving time for this offense? _____ Yes _____ No

25. Longer or shorter than your term?
    _____ longer   _____ shorter   _____ same
    _____ DK   _____ N/A

26. Were you represented by legal counsel during your trial?

    _____ Yes—public defender/state-appointed
    _____ Yes—private counsel
    _____ No

27. What sentence did you receive?

    _____ 6 months or less   _____ less than 1 year
    _____ 1 year–2 yrs, 11 mo   _____ 3 yrs–5 yrs, 11 mo
    _____ 6 yrs–9 yrs, 11 mo   _____ 10 yrs–14 yrs, 11 mo
    _____ 15 yrs–19 yrs, 11 mo   _____ 20 yrs–29 yrs, 11 mo
    _____ over 30 years   _____ 7 to life
    _____ 15 to life   _____ 15+–20 to life
    _____ 20+–30 to life   _____ 30+ and over to life
    _____ life w/ possibility of parole _____ life plus
    _____ LWOP   _____ Condemned
    _____ Other   _____ don't know

CHILDREN

28. Do you have children? _____ Yes _____ No (If no ⇒ Q#43)

    If yes:
29. How many children do you have? _____

30. Ages: _____

31. Do you have legal custody of your child(ren)?

    _____ Yes/all   _____ Yes/some   _____ No
    _____ D K   _____ N/A

32. Where are your children now living? _____
    _____

33. How far away from this prison does your child (who lives the farthest) live? _____

34. Were any of your children living with you right before you were arrested?

    _____ Yes—all of them   _____ Yes—some of them
    _____ no—kids elsewhere   _____ No—kids grown
    _____ N/A, D/K

35. Did any of your children witness your arrest?
    _____ Yes _____ No

36. When you were first arrested, what happened to your children?

    _____ N/A
    _____ Police allowed me to make arrangements with family
    _____ Police allowed me to make arrangements with friends
    _____ Children were taken to police station with me
    _____ CPS/social worker took them
    _____ They were already in other's custody
    _____ Children didn't live with me
    _____ Don't know
    _____ Other

VISITING/CONTACT

We are interested in how much contact you might have with your family, your children, and friends. These next questions ask about that contact.

Codes:
1. 4 or more times per week
2. 1-3 times per week
3. every 2 weeks or so
4. every 3 weeks or so
5. about once a month
6. every 2 months or so
7. every 3 months or so
8. between 4 and 6 months
9. longer than 6 months
10. sporadic—no pattern, but some contact
11. never since this incarceration
12. not able due to rules/custody
13. don't know
14. pending visiting approval
15. not eligible—status added elsewhere
16. paper work in process
17. rules prohibit contact
18. no partner
19. cannot call this person
20. no friends/family
99. N/A

37. Since you have been here, how often do you call your children?
_____

38 Since you have been here, how often do you receive letters from your children? _____

39. Since you have been here, how often do you write letters to your children? _____

40. Since you have been here, how often do you have regular visits with your children? _____

41. Since you have been here, how often do you have FLU visits with your children?   _____

42. (If children never visit) Can you tell me some of the reasons your children do not visit?   _____   _____   _____

 Codes:
   1. too far
   2. caregiver won't bring because too far
   3. caregiver won't bring/doesn't want to
   4. I do not want them here
   5. children too young to be here
   6. too expensive to travel
   7. transportation problems
   8. child doesn't know I'm here
   9. don't know
  10. children do visit
  11. paper work not processed
  12. not eligible
  99. N/A

   _____ most important   _____ third
   _____ second most   _____ fourth

43. Is there someone on the outside/not here with you that you consider as your partner and would like to have contact with?
   _____ Yes   _____ No

44. Are you in contact with that person?

   _____ person on street: yes—through calls, letters, etc.
   _____ person on street: no contact
   _____ person in jail/prison: have contact through friends/family
   _____ person in jail/prison: no contact
   _____ other?
   _____ N/A

Codes:

1. 4 or more times per week	12. not able due to
2. 1–3 times per week	rules/custody
3. every 2 weeks or so	13. don't know
4. every 3 weeks or so	14. pending visiting approval
5. about once a month	15. not eligible—status
6. every 2 months or so	added elsewhere
7. every 3 months or so	16. paper work still
8. between 4 and 6 months	in process
9. longer than 6 months	17. rules prohibit contact
10. sporadic—no pattern,	18. no partner
but some contact	19. cannot call this person
11. never since this	20. no friends/family
incarceration	99. N/A

45. Since you have been here, how often do you call your partner?
_____

46. Since you have been here, how often do you receive letters from your partner?   _____

47. Since you have been here, how often do you write to your partner?   _____

48. Since you have been here, how often do you have regular visits with your partner?   _____

49. Are you eligible for FLU visits with your partner?
_____ Yes   _____ No

_____ no partner
_____ not married
_____ married but spouse imprisoned
_____ married but spouse ineligible

50. Since you have been here, how often do you have FLU visits with your partner?   _____

51. Since you have been here, how often do you call your other family members or friends?   _____

52. Since you have been here, how often do you receive letters from your other family members/ friends?   _____

53. Since you have been here, how often do you write letters to your other family members/ friends?   _____

54. Since you have been here, how often do you have regular visits with your other family members or friends?   _____

55. Since you have been here, how often do you have FLU visits with your other family members or friends?   _____

ABUSE HISTORY

Codes for frequency:
1. a one time event
2. more than once
   but not ongoing

3. an ongoing,
   recurrent event
99. N/A

Codes for abuser / perpetrator:
1. father
2. step-father
3. mother
4. step-mother
5. mother's boyfriend
6. your boyfriend
7. spouse/partner
8. other male relative
   (exc. brother)
9. other female relative
10. brother
99. N/A

11. sister
12. step-brother
13. step-sister
14. sibling's peers
15. your peers
16. family friend/neighbor
17. authority figure
    (teacher, etc.)
18. stranger
19. other _____
20. didn't know who they were

As a child:

56. Were you ever physically abused/harmed/hit?
    _____ Yes   _____ No

If yes:
57. How often did this occur?   _____

58. Can you tell me all the people who may have hurt you?

    _____   _____   _____   _____   _____   _____   _____

59. Were you ever sexually abused?   _____ Yes   _____ No

    If yes:
60. How often did this occur?   _____

61. Can you tell me all the people who may have sexually abused
    you?   _____   _____   _____   _____   _____   _____

62. Were you ever emotionally abused or neglected?
    _____ Yes   _____ No

    If yes:
63. How often did this occur?   _____

64. Can you tell me all the people who may have abused/neglected
    you?   _____   _____   _____   _____   _____   _____

65. Were you ever sexually assaulted?   _____ Yes   _____ No

    If yes:
66. How often did this occur?   _____

67. Can you tell me all the people who may have assaulted you?

    _____   _____   _____   _____   _____   _____   _____

As an adult:

68. Were you ever physically abused/battered?
    _____ Yes   _____ No

    If yes:
69. How often did this occur?   _____

70. Can you tell me all the people who may have hurt you?

    _____   _____   _____   _____   _____   _____   _____

71. Were you ever sexually abused?   _____ Yes   _____ No

    If yes:
72. How often did this occur?   _____

73. Can you tell me all the people who may have sexually abused you? _____ _____ _____ _____ _____ _____

74. Were you ever emotionally abused/ neglected?
_____ Yes _____ No

If yes:
75. How often did this occur? _____

76. Can you tell me all the people who may have abused/neglected you? _____ _____ _____ _____ _____ _____

77. Were you ever sexually assaulted? _____ Yes _____ No

If yes:
78. How often did this occur? _____

79. Can you tell me all the people who may have assaulted you?

_____ _____ _____ _____ _____ _____ _____

80. You have told me about some things that have happened to you as a child. Do you feel this has had anything to do with your reasons for committing the crime?

_____ Yes _____ No
_____ don't know _____ N/A

81. Have you received counseling for abuse while serving your term?

_____ Yes _____ No
_____ don't know _____ N/A

82. Would you like to receive counseling or participate in a program dealing with surviving abuse?

_____ Yes _____ No _____ DK
_____ no interest/need _____ N/A

83. Do you feel that any counseling you have received has helped?

_____ Yes _____ No _____ N/A
_____ never received counseling
_____ never needed counseling

ALCOHOL/DRUG USE HISTORY

Codes:
1. Twice a day or more
2. Daily or almost daily
3. 3-5 times a week
4. Once or twice a week
5. Week-ends
6. Once every 2-3 weeks
7. Every month or two
8. Less than once every 3-4 mos
9. Occasional/sporadic
10. Binge pattern
11. Never
99. N/A

84. Have you ever used alcohol?   _____ Yes   _____ No

Was alcohol use ever a problem in your life?
_____ Yes   _____ No

Did you drink alcohol the last year you were free?
_____ Yes   _____ No

If so, how often? (use code)   _____

85. Have you ever used illegal drugs?   _____ Yes   _____ No

Were illegal drugs ever a problem in your life?
_____ Yes   _____ No

Did you use illegal drugs the last year you were free?
_____ Yes   _____ No

If so, how often? (use code)   _____

What illegal drugs did you use most often?   _____
_____

86. Have you ever used prescription drugs?
_____ Yes   _____ No

Were Rx drugs ever a problem in your life?
_____ Yes   _____ No

Did you use Rx drugs the last year you were free?
_____ Yes   _____ No

If so, how often? (use code)   _____

What Rx drugs did you use most often?

_____

Did you ever drink alcohol while using Rx drugs?
_____ Yes _____ No

87. How old were you when you first drank alcohol?
_____ _____ N/A

88. How old were you when you first used drugs?
_____ _____ N/A

89. How old were you when you first used Rx drugs?
_____ _____ N/A

LIFE INSIDE

90. Which programs (other than a job) do you participate in?
_____ _____ _____

1. vocational	8. self-help
2. educational	9. religious groups
3. legal	10. recreational
4. individual counseling	11. drug/alcohol
5. group counseling	12. arts/crafts/music
6. parenting	13. other
7. lifer group	99. No participation

specific programs: _____

91. Which of these programs has been helpful/beneficial to you?

_____

92. What is your current assignment?

_____ Food service	_____ Other services (laundry)
_____ Library, stockroom, etc.	_____ Orderly/Porter
_____ Industries/PIA	_____ Vocational Training
_____ Educational	_____ Landscape/Yard Crew
_____ Clerk	_____ Warehouse
_____ Outside Crew	_____ Joint Venture
_____ Other	_____ No job

93. Where do you spend the bulk of your free time here?

_____ in my room   _____ in the day room
_____ in the unit   _____ on the yard
_____ in the library   _____ at hobby craft
_____ in the gym   _____ the chapel
_____ no one place   _____ Other

94. Do you shop (go to the canteen)?
_____ Yes   _____ No   _____ N/A

95. Where does your commissary money come from?

_____ my parents/relatives   _____ my friends
_____ my children   _____ my partner
_____ own income/earned here   _____ trading
_____ own income/from outside _____ N/A, DK
_____ no single source   _____ do not shop

96. Do you ever receive packages for your own use?
_____ Yes   _____ No

97. How often?

_____ every quarter   _____ 3 times a year
_____ twice a year   _____ once a year
_____ less than once a year but sometimes
_____ no pattern   _____ never
_____ N/A

98. Have you ever been indigent in here?
_____ Yes   _____ No   _____ In the past

99. How many 115s have you been found guilty of?   _____

HEALTH QUESTIONS

100. Do you have any health conditions that require attention?
_____ Yes   _____ No

101. Which conditions do you have? (Ask for each condition if receiving adequate attention.)

Codes:
1. have condition and receiving adequate attention
2. have condition and receiving inadequate attention
3. do not have condition

_____ Blood problems (anemia, sickle cell, lupus, etc.)
_____ Asthma/bronchitis
_____ Cancer
_____ Diabetes
_____ Aneurysm
_____ TB
_____ Heart conditions
_____ Epilepsy
_____ STD
_____ HIV/AIDS +
_____ HIV/AIDS—symptoms
_____ gynecological/menstrual problems
_____ pregnancy
_____ post-partum
_____ back problems
_____ arthritis
_____ knee or other joint problems
_____ mental/emotional problems
_____ regulation of psychotropic drugs
_____ physical disability
_____ menopause
_____ other _____

QUESTIONNAIRE II—FOLLOW-UP

THIS QUESTIONNAIRE IS COMPLETELY CONFIDENTIAL. DO *NOT* WRITE YOUR NAME OR NUMBER ON THIS QUESTION-NAIRE. *THANK YOU FOR YOUR HELP.*

Please answer the following questions as best you can. Feel free to add any information that you think is important. You can write on the back of these pages.

This first set of questions has to do with the abusive relationship that resulted in your being in prison.

1. What was *your age* when you first got involved with this man?
   _____ years old.

2. What was *his age* when you first got involved with him?
   _____ years old.

3. What was *his* race / ethnicity?

   _____ African American   _____ Asian/Pacific Islander
   _____ Latino / Hispanic   _____ Native American
   _____ White   _____ Other _____

4. How long were the two of you involved?   _____ years.

5. During your time together, did this man have a problem with alcohol and / or drugs?

   YES _____   NO _____

6. Some women who were abused report a past problem with alcohol and/or drugs, was this a problem for you *during* your time with this man?

   YES _____   NO _____ (Go to # 8)
   ↓

7. Was this a problem for you before you became involved with this man?

   YES _____   NO _____

8. What was *his* major occupation / source of income?

_____

9. Was *he* ever arrested?

YES _____ NO _____ (Go to # 10)
↓
If you answered YES, what was the charge or charges?

_____

_____

10. Did his abuse give you any *injuries*?

YES _____ NO _____ (Go to # 16)

11. List any injuries, temporary or permanent, caused by his abuse. You may include physical, sexual, or mental harm.

_____

_____

_____

_____

_____
↓
12. Did you receive professional medical attention for any of these injuries?

YES _____ NO _____ (Go to # 16)
↓
13. Did medical personnel know that you were the victim of domestic violence?

YES _____ NO _____ (Go to # 16)
↓
14. Did they report the abuse?

YES _____ NO _____ (Go to # 16)
↓
15. What happened? _____

_____

_____

_____

_____

16. Were children in the home during this relationship?

    YES _____   NO _____ (Go to # 23)
    ↓

17. Did he ever abuse any of your *children*?

    YES _____   NO _____ (Go to # 22)
    ↓

    If you answered yes, what kind of child abuse?
18. Physical Abuse:

    _____ once   _____ more than once   _____ ongoing

19. Sexual Abuse:

    _____ once   _____ more than once   _____ ongoing

20. Emotional Abuse:

    _____ once   _____ more than once   _____ ongoing

21. Death Threats:

    _____ once   _____ more than once   _____ ongoing

22. Did your children witness or know about his violence against
    you?

    YES _____   NO _____

23. Did he ever threaten to kill members of your family or other
    loved ones?

    YES _____   NO _____ (Go to # 26)
    ↓

24. If you answered *yes*, who did he threaten?   _____

    _____
    ↓

25. If you answered *yes*, who knew about the threat?

    _____
    _____
    _____

Sometimes women who are abused try different things to stop the violence. Did you ever:

26. Try to get a restraining order?   YES _____   NO _____
27. Take out a restraining order?   YES _____   NO _____
28. File for divorce?   YES _____   NO _____
29. Get a divorce?   YES _____   NO _____
30. File for separation?   YES _____   NO _____
31. Get a separation?   YES _____   NO _____
32. File charges against him?   YES _____   NO _____
33. Have him arrested?   YES _____   NO _____
34. Call 911 when he abused you?   YES _____   NO _____
35. Move out of the home?   YES _____   NO _____
36. Move *him* out of the home?   YES _____   NO _____
37. *Try* to hide from him, leave, or run away?
    YES _____   NO _____

If you marked NO to *all* these actions, go to # 39

38. If you marked *yes* to any part of the last set of questions, please describe in a few words what happened after you took the action(s). _____

_____

_____

_____

_____

_____

39 Sometimes women who are abused try to get help from others. Was this true in your case?

YES _____ (Go to #41)   NO _____
                                    ↓

40. If *no*, can you tell me in a few words what may have prevented you getting outside help? _____

_____

_____

_____

_____

_____

41. If you answered *yes*, where did you look for help? About how
    many times? Please mark all that apply.

_____ police	_____ time(s)
_____ courts / judge	_____ time(s)
_____ religious leader	_____ time(s)
_____ doctor / nurse	_____ time(s)
_____ counselor / therapist	_____ time(s)
_____ support group	_____ time(s)
_____ lawyer	_____ time(s)
_____ woman's shelter	_____ time(s)
_____ family	_____ time(s)
_____ other: please describe _____	

42 If you checked any of the above, please describe in a few words
    what happened when you made that contact.   _____

    _____
    _____
    _____
    _____
    _____
    _____
    _____

This next set of questions has to do with the homicide. *Thank you* for
taking the time to answer these questions.

43. On the *day* of the incident, before the homicide, had you been in
    contact with the police?

    YES _____   NO _____ (Go to # 45)
    ↓

44. Briefly, what happened during that earlier contact with the
    police?   _____

    _____
    _____
    _____
    _____
    _____
    _____
    _____
    _____

45. At the time of the homicide, what was going on in the relation-ship?

_____ trying to end the relationship
_____ trying to leave when the homicide occurred
_____ already separated or divorced
_____ nothing new, things were pretty much as they had always been
_____ other (describe) _____

46. What was *your age* when the homicide occurred? _____ years

47. What was the *year* of the incident? 19 _____.

48. In what city or county did it occur? _____

49. Who reported the homicide? _____

50. What was the *year* of your arrest? 19 _____

51. Did the arrest happen right away?

YES _____ (Go to # 53) NO _____
$\downarrow$

52. How much time went by before you were arrested?

_____

53. Were you at the scene when the homicide occurred?

YES _____ NO _____

54. When the homicide occurred, was anyone under the influence of *alcohol or drugs*?
$\downarrow$
YES _____ NO _____ (Go to # 56)

55. If yes, *who* was under the influence? _____

56. Was anyone else charged with the crime besides you?
$\downarrow$
YES _____ NO _____ (Go to # 58)

57. If you answered yes, please identify your codefendant(s)?

    _____ child(ren)   Who? (son) _____
    _____ family member Who? (brother?) _____
    _____ friend   Who? (neighbor?) _____
    _____ other   Who? _____

This last set of questions relates to jail, trial, or plea bargains.

58. During your time in *jail*, were you given drugs such as tranquilizers or anti-depressants?

    YES _____   NO _____ (Go to # 62)
    ↓

59. *Who* decided you needed this medication?   _____

    _____
    ↓

60. *What kind* of drugs did they give you?   _____

    _____
    ↓

61. Did *you* want to be given this medication?

    YES _____   NO _____

62. How was your case handled?

    _____ The case was plea bargained (Go to # 63)
    _____ A plea was offered and it was turned down. The case went
           to trial (Go to # 64)
    _____ The case went to trial and no plea was offered. (Go to
           # 64)

63. If your case was plea bargained, what did the prosecutor tell you about your choices?   _____

    _____ (Go to # 72)

For those who went to trial:

64. Did you testify at your trial?   YES _____   NO _____

65. Was this your only trial for this incident?

    YES _____ (Go to # 68)   NO _____

66. If NO, how many times did your case go to trial?   _____
    ↓
67. Please explain what happened in your earlier trial(s)

    _____

    _____

    _____

    _____

    _____

68. During the trial that ended with this conviction, were you given *drugs* such as tranquilizers or anti-depressants?

    YES _____   NO _____ (Go to # 70)
    ↓
69. What kind of drugs?   _____

    _____

70. How long did your trial last?   _____

71. If you know, what was your defense based on? (self-defense?)

    _____

72. Where did the case take place? (city or county)   _____

    _____

73. What year did your case take place?   19 _____

74. Did any evidence of his abuse enter into your trial?

    YES _____   NO _____

75. Was your lawyer male or female?

    _____ male   _____ female

76. Was the prosecutor male or female?

    _____ male   _____ female

77. Was the judge male or female?

_____ male   _____ female

Thank you for taking the time to fill out this questionnaire. If you want to add any other information, please write in the space below and on the back of these pages.

Appendix C

INTERVIEW GUIDE

What was it like for you growing up in your home? What was your parents' marriage like? How did they act toward you/discipline you? How did you see yourself as a little girl? Did you see or experience any abuse or violence?

What happened the first time that you experienced violence, either as a child or adult? Did any prior marriage or relationship with men involve abuse? Can you tell me about it? How did the relationship end?

What attracted you to your last partner/spouse? Was there violence in the dating relationship? Do you know if he had been violent with anyone else? What was he like with you when he wasn't being violent? How were decisions made, e.g. finances, children, use of time? How were disagreements handled? Any substance abuse? Were you aware if he had an arrest record?

I'd like to ask some questions about the first violent episode with this man. How long had you been together? What happened? What went on in your mind? Who did you hold responsible? Were you injured? What did you do? Did you think about leaving him? Did you tell anyone? Call the police? Get medical care? Seek counseling? What did he do afterwards?

How often did beatings occur? Increase over time? How long did they go on? During pregnancy? What was typical? Weapons? Did you see a pattern to his violence? What was in it for him? Was sexual abuse ever part of his violence or intimidation? What kinds of injuries have you experienced and what was done about them? Did you ever try to end the marriage/ relationship? What happened? Did you consider yourself a "battered woman?" Did you ever think about or attempt suicide?

Who else knew about the abuse? How did they know? Was there any outside intervention? Family; friends; medical worker; mental health worker; religious advisor; police; prosecutor...? What was done? What was the attitude of others towards you? Towards him?

Was he abusive with anyone else? What threats did he ever make against you/children/family members? Did he make direct attempts on your life? Did you ever threaten him? How?

Can you describe what happened that resulted in the death of your abuser? Why did the homicide occur at that particular time? What about the homicide situation was different from previous provoking episodes? How old were you when this occurred? How long with him?

What happened immediately after he died? How did the police treat you when they became involved? When were you charged and what was the charge? What went on inside you?

Tell me about your experience with the criminal justice system as a woman accused of killing her partner/spouse. Was your lawyer familiar with the dynamics of battering? Did you go to trial or take a plea? Was an expert witness used in your defense? Was evidence of past abuse considered? Was the disposition of your case reasonable to you? What was the outcome? What was the jurisdiction and year of your trial?

When were you sent to prison? What was it like for you when you first got here? Was there a change in your ideas about who you were? What is it like for you now? What is the most negative thing about being here? Anything positive? What do you do to maintain your sense of self/individuality in prison? Have you gone before the parole board? What happened?

What is your definition of a "battered woman?" When did you first define yourself as a "battered woman?" What do you get out of being a member of CWAA and attending meetings?

What would you say to women who are still in relationship with abusive men? Is there anything that you would do differently if you had it to do over?

Notes

*Chapter Two. Battered Women Who Kill
and the Criminal Justice System*

1. Common stereotypes include: battered women choose to stay in abusive relationships and could leave if they wanted to; women provoke the beating and probably deserve to be hit; abused women will drop charges against their attackers; domestic violence is a private rather than criminal issue and is not as serious as violence outside the home; domestic violence is a way of life for some people; the man is the sole head of the household and the wife should obey him.

2. Common stereotypes include: she is lying, vengeful, jealous, masochistic; thus, she probably does not qualify for a plea of self-defense.

Chapter Five. A Profile of Convicted Survivors

1. In 1995, America's rate of incarceration was 600 per 100,000 (The Sentencing Project 1997).

2. This is an average taken from the percentage of women reporting problem use with given illegal drugs.

3. One woman was also found guilty of conspiracy (86).

4. Four women were also convicted on conspiracy charges (86).

5. In Bannister's research, only five out of 275 cases were not intraracial.

Chapter Nine. Coercive Drugging

1. Frequently mentioned antidepressants and antipsychotics include: Mellaril, Elavil, Desyrel, Triavil, Vivactil, Vistaril, Haldol, Lithium, Stelazine, Sinequan, and Thorazine.

Chapter Eleven. Conclusion and Policy Implications

1. As of November 1996, California inmates without parole dates are not allowed quarterly overnight visits with immediate family members.

References

Abbott, Jack Henry. 1981. *In the belly of the beast*. New York: Random House.

Abbott, Jean, Robin Johnson, Jane Koziol-McLain, and Steven R. Lowenstein. 1995. Domestic violence against women: Incidence and prevalence in an emergency department population. *Journal of the American Medical Association* 273:1763–1767.

Abel, Eileen Mazur, and Edward K. Suh. 1987. Use of police services by battered women. *Social Work* 32 (Nov–Dec): 526–528.

American Bar Association Commission on Domestic Violence. 1997. *When will they ever learn? Educating to end domestic violence: A law school report*. Chicago: American Bar Association.

American Medical Association. 1992. *Diagnostic and treatment guidelines on domestic violence*. Chicago: American Medical Association.

American Psychiatric Association. 1994. *Diagnostic and statistical manual of mental disorders IV*. Washington, DC: American Psychiatric Association.

Amnesty International. 1973. *Report on torture*. New York: Farrar, Straus & Giroux.

Andersen, Margaret L. 2000. *Thinking about women 5/e*. Boston: Allyn and Bacon.

Andersen, Susan M., Teresa Ramirez Boulette, and Amy H. Schwartz. 1991. Psychological maltreatment of spouses. In *Case studies in family violence*, ed. Robert T. Ammerman and Michel Hersen. New York: Plenum Press.

Archer, Naomi Hilton. 1989. Battered women and the legal system: Past, present, and future. *Law and Psychology Review* 13:145–163.

Attorney General's Task Force on Family Violence. 1984. *Final report*. Washington, DC: U.S. Department of Justice.

Auerhahn, Kathleen, and Elizabeth Dermody Leonard. 2000. Docile bodies? Chemical restraints and the female inmate. *The Journal of Criminal Law and Criminology* 90(2):599–634.

Austin, James, Barbara Bloom, and Trish Donahue. 1992. *Female offenders in the community: An analysis of innovative strategies and programs*. San Francisco: National Council on Crime and Delinquency.

Bachman, Ronet. 1994. *Violence against women*. Washington, DC: U.S. Department of Justice.

———, and Linda E. Saltzman. 1995. *Violence against women: Estimates from the redesigned survey*. Washington, DC: U.S. Department of Justice.

Bannister, Shelley A. 1991. The criminalization of women fighting back against male abuse: Imprisoned battered women as political prisoners. *Humanity & Society* 15:400–416.

———. 1993. Battered women who kill their abusers: Their courtroom battles. In *It's a crime: Women and justice*, ed. Roslyn Muraskin and Ted Alleman. Englewood Cliffs, NJ: Regents/Prentice-Hall.

———. 1996. Battered women who kill: Status and situational determinants of courtroom outcomes. Ph.D. dissertation, Department of Sociology, University of Illinois at Chicago.

Beck, Allen J. 2000. *Prisoners in 1999*. Washington, DC: U.S. Department of Justice.

Beck, Allen J., and Jennifer C. Karberg. 2001. Prison and jail inmates at midyear 2000. Washington, DC: U.S. Department of Justice.

———, and Christopher J. Mumola. 1999. *Prisoners in 1998*. Washington, DC: U.S. Department of Justice.

Belknap, Joanne. 1995. Law enforcement officers' attitudes about the appropriate responses to woman battering. *International Review of Victimology* 4:47–62.

———. 2001. *The invisible woman: Gender, crime, and justice 2/e*. Belmont, CA: Wadsworth.

Bell, Robinette, Mary Duncan, Julia Eilenberg, Mindy Fullilove, Denise Hein, Lorraine Innes, Lisa Mellman, and Paula Panzer. 1996. *Violence against women in the United States: A comprehensive background paper*. New York: The Commonwealth Fund.

Bergen, Raquel Kennedy. 1999. Marital rape. Available online. http://www.vawnet.org/vnl/library/general/libraryrecord1095.htm.

———. 1993. Interviewing survivors of marital rape. In *Researching sensitive topics*, ed. Claire M. Renzetti and Raymond M. Lee. Newbury Park, CA: Sage.

Bernat, Frances. 2001. Gender and law. In *Women, crime, and criminal justice*, ed. Claire M. Renzetti and Lynne Goodstein. Los Angeles: Roxbury.

Block, Carolyn Rebecca, and Antigone Christakos. 1995. Intimate partner homicide in Chicago over 29 years. *Crime & Delinquency* 41:496–526.

Bloom, Barbara E. 1996. *Triple jeopardy: Race, class, and gender as factors in women's imprisonment.* Ph.D. dissertation, Department of Sociology. University of California, Riverside.

Bloom, Barbara, Meda Chesney-Lind, and Barbara Owen. 1994. Women in California prisons: Hidden victims of the war on drugs. San Francisco: Center for Juvenile and Criminal Justice.

Bograd, Michele. 1984. Family systems approaches to wife battering: A feminist critique. *American Journal of Orthopsychiatry* 54:558–568.

Bonczar, Thomas P., and Lauren E. Glaze. 1999. *Probation and parole in the United States, 1998.* Washington, DC: U.S. Department of Justice.

Bourg, Sherrie, and Harley V. Stock. 1999. A review of domestic violence statistics in a police department using a pro-arrest policy: Are pro-arrest policies enough? In *Family violence: Studies from the social sciences and professions, vol 2: Relationship violence 2/e*, ed. James M. Makepeace. New York: McGraw-Hill.

Bowker, Lee H. 1987. Battered women as consumers of legal services: Reports from a national survey. *Response* 10 (1): 10–17.

———. 1993. A battered woman's problems are social, not psychological. In *Current controversies on family violence*, ed. Richard J. Gelles and Donileen R. Loseke. Newbury Park, CA: Sage.

Braun, Judith V., and Steven Lipson. 1993. *Toward a restraint-free environment: Reducing the use of physical and chemical restraints in long-term and acute care settings.* Baltimore: Health Professions Press.

Brown, Michael P., and James E. Hendricks. 1998. Wife abuse. In *Violence in intimate relationships*, ed. Nicky Ali Jackson and Gisele Casanova Oates. Boston: Butterworth-Heinemann.

Browne, Angela. 1987. *When battered women kill.* New York: Free Press.

———. 1988. Family homicide: When victimized women kill. In *Handbook on family violence*, ed. Vincent B. Van Hasselt, Randall L. Morrison, Alan S. Bellack, and Michel Hersen. New York: Plenum.

———. 1992. Violence against women: Relevance for medical practitioners. *Journal of the American Medical Association* 267:3184–3189.

———. 1995. Fear and the perception of alternatives: Asking "Why battered women don't leave" is the wrong question. In *The criminal justice system and women*, ed. Barbara Raffel Price and Natalie J. Sokoloff. New York: McGraw-Hill.

——, and Kirk R. Williams. 1989. Exploring the effect of resource availability and the likelihood of female-perpetrated homicides. *Law & Society Review* 23:75–94.

Brownstein, Henry H., Barry J. Spunt, Susan Crimmins, Paul J. Goldstein, and Sandra Langley. 1994. Changing patterns of lethal violence by women: A research note. *Women & Criminal Justice* 5:99–116.

Buzawa, Eve S., and Carl G. Buzawa. 1993. The impact of arrest on domestic violence: introduction. *American Behavioral Scientist* 36(5): 558–574.

——. 1996. *Domestic violence: The criminal justice response.* Thousand Oaks, CA: Sage.

Buzawa, Eve, Thomas L. Austin, and Carl G. Buzawa. 1995. Responding to crimes of violence against women: Gender differences versus organizational imperatives. *Crime & Delinquency* 41:443–466.

California Department of Corrections. 1999. *Population reports.* Retrieved September 6, 1999 http://www.cdc.state.ca.us/reports/monthpop.htm.

——. 2000. Retrieved August 1, 2000 http//www.cdc.state.ca.us/facility/facil.htm.

Campbell, Jacquelyn C. 1992. "If I can't have you, no one can": Power and control in homicide of female partners. In *Femicide: The politics of woman killing*, ed. J. Radford and D. E. H. Russell. New York: Twayne.

——. 1995. Prediction of homicide of and by battered women. In *Assessing dangerousness: Violence by sexual offenders, batterers, and child abusers*, ed. Jacquelyn C. Campbell. Thousand Oaks, CA: Sage.

——. 1996. Beth Sipe and the health care system. In *I am not your victim*, ed. Beth Sipe and Evelyn J. Hall. Thousand Oaks, CA: Sage.

Caringella-MacDonald, Susan. 1997. Women victimized by private violence. In *Violence between intimate partners*, ed. Albert P. Cardarelli. Boston: Allyn and Bacon.

Casenave, Noel A., and Margaret Zahn. 1992. Women, murder and male domination: Police reports of domestic violence in Chicago and Philadelphia. In *Intimate violence: Interdisciplinary perspectives*, ed. Emilio Viano. Washington, DC: Hemisphere Publishing.

Castel, Jacqueline R. 1990. Discerning justice for battered women who kill. *University of Toronto Faculty of Law Review* 49 (2): 229–258.

Chalke, Frank C. 1978. Prison psychiatrists: A survey of ethical guidelines. *Psychiatric Annals* 8:63–77.

Chesney-Lind, Meda. 1995. Rethinking women's imprisonment: A critical examination of trends in female incarceration. In *The criminal justice system and women*, ed. Barbara Raffel Price and Natalie J. Sokoloff. New York: McGraw-Hill.

Chimbos, Peter D. 1978. *Marital violence: A study of interspouse homicide*. San Francisco: R & E Research Associates.

Clear, Todd R., and George F. Cole. 1997. *American corrections* 4/e. Belmont, CA: Wadsworth.

Collins, Karen Scott, Cathy Schoen, Susan Joseph, Lisa Duchon, Elisabeth Simantov, and Michele Yellowitz. 1999. 1998 Survey of Women's Health. New York: Commonwealth Fund.

Coronado, Michael. 2000. Emotional services welcome her home. The Press Enterprise. December 12, 2000.

Crites, Laura L. 1987. Wife abuse: The judicial record. In *Women, the courts, and equality*, ed. Laura L. Crites and Winifred L. Hepperle. Newbury Park, CA: Sage.

Crowe, Ann H. 1996. Stopping terrorism at home. *Annual editions: Criminal justice 96/97*. Guilford, CT: Dushkin.

Crowell, Nancy A., and Ann W. Burgess, eds. 1996. *Understanding violence against women*. Washington, DC: National Academy Press.

Culliver, Concetta C. 1993. Females behind prison bars. In *Female criminality: The state of the art*, ed. Concetta C. Culliver. New York: Garland.

Currie, Elliot. 1998. *Crime and punishment in America*. New York: Henry Holt.

Daly, Kathleen, and Meda Chesney-Lind. 1988. Feminism and criminology. *Justice Quarterly* 5:499–535.

Davidson, Terry. 1977. Wifebeating: A recurring phenomenon throughout history. In *Battered women*, ed. Maria Roy. New York: Van Nostrand Reinhold.

Dawson, John M., and Patrick A. Langan. 1994. *Murder in families*. Washington, DC: U.S. Department of Justice.

Dawson, Myrna, and Rosemary Gartner. 1998. Differences in the characteristics of intimate femicides. *Homicide Studies* 2 (4): 378–399.

Diaz, Katherine. 1996. *Pathfinder on domestic violence with emphasis on the criminal justice system*. New York: Center on Crime, Communities, & Culture. http://www.soros.org/crime/dvpath.html.

Dingerson, Leigh. 1991. Women on death row. *Response* 14:5–6.

Dobash, R. Emerson, and Russell Dobash. 1977. Love, honor, and obey: Institutional ideologies and the struggle for battered women. *Contemporary Crises* 1:403–415.

———. 1979. *Violence against wives*. New York: Free Press.

———. 1988. Research as social action: The struggle for battered women. In *Feminist perspectives on wife abuse*, ed. Kirsti Yllo and Michele Bograd. Newbury Park, CA: Sage.

———. 1992. Women, violence, and social change. London: Routledge.

Dobash, Russell, R. Emerson Dobash, Margo Wilson, and Martin Daly. 1999. The myth of sexual symmetry in marital violence. In *Family violence: Studies from the social sciences and professions, vol. 2: Relationship violence 2/e*, ed. James M. Makepeace. New York: McGraw-Hill.

Doerner, William G., and Steven P. Lab. 1998. *Victimology*. Cincinnati: Anderson.

Du Bois, B. 1983. Passionate scholarship: Notes on values, knowing and method in feminist social science. In *Theories of women's studies*, ed. Gloria Bowles and Renate Duelli Klein. London: Routledge and Kegan Paul.

Duncan, Jane W., and Glen M. Duncan. 1978. Murder in the family. In *Violence: Perspectives on murder and aggression*, ed. Irwin Kutash, Samuel Kutash, and Louis Schlesinger. Chapel Hill: University of North Carolina.

Durkheim, Emile. 1897/1951. *Suicide: A study of sociology*. Trans. George Simpson. Glencoe, IL: The Free Press.

Edwards, Rosalind. 1993. An education in interviewing. In *Researching sensitive topics*, ed. Claire M. Renzetti and Raymond M. Lee. Newbury Park, CA: Sage.

Edwards, Susan S. M. 1985. A socio-legal evaluation of gender ideologies in domestic violence assault and spousal homicides. *Victimology: An International Journal* 10:186–205.

Eisenberg, Alan D., and David A. Dillon. 1989. Medico-legal aspects of representing the battered woman. In *Representing . . . Battered women who kill*, ed. Sara Lee Johann and Frank Osanka. Springfield, IL: Charles C. Thomas.

Ellis, Desmond, and Walter S. DeKeseredy. 1997. Rethinking estrangement, interventions, and intimate femicide. *Violence against women* 3:590–609.

Ewing, Charles Patrick. 1987. *Battered women who kill*. Lexington, MA: Lexington Books.

———. 1990. Psychological self-defense: A proposed justification for battered women who kill. *Law and Human Behavior* 14:579–594.

———. 1997. *Fatal families*. Thousand Oaks, CA: Sage.

Fagan, Jeffrey. 1996.*The criminalization of domestic violence: Promises and limits*. Washington, DC: U.S. Department of Justice.

Ferguson, Carroy U. 1998. Dating violence as a social phenomenon. In *Violence in intimate relationships*, ed. Nicky Ali Jackson and Gisele Casanova Oates. Boston, MA: Butterworth-Heinemann.

Ferraro, Kathleen J. 1989. Policing woman battering. *Social Problems* 36:61–74.

———. 1993. Cops, courts, and woman battering. In *Violence against women: The bloody footprints*, ed. Pauline B. Bart and Eileen G. Moran. Newbury Park, CA: Sage.

———. 1997. Battered women: Strategies for survival. In *Violence between intimate partners*, ed. Albert P. Cardarelli. Boston: Allyn and Bacon.

———. 2001. Women battering: More than a family problem. In *Women, crime, and criminal justice*, ed. Claire M. Renzetti and Lynne Goodstein. Los Angeles: Roxbury.

———, and John M. Johnson. 1983. How women experience battering: The process of victimization. *Social Problems* 30:325–339.

Fine, Michelle. 1995. The politics of research and activism: Violence against women. In *The criminal justice system and women*, ed. Barbara Raffel Price and Natalie J. Sokoloff. New York: McGraw-Hill.

Finn, Peter, and Sarah Colson. 1990. *Civil protection orders: Legislation, current court practice, and enforcement*. Washington, DC: National Institute of Justice. March 1990 NCJ 123263.

Flitcraft, Anne H. 1995. Clinical violence intervention: Lessons from battered women. *Journal of Health Care for the Poor and Underserved* 6:187–195.

Foster, Lynne A., Christine Mann Veale, and Catherine Ingram Fogel. 1989. Factors present when battered women kill. *Issues in Mental Health Nursing* 10:273–284.

Friedman, Lucy N., and Minna Shulman. 1990. Domestic violence: The criminal justice response. In *Victims of crime: Problems, policies, and programs*, ed. Arthur J. Lurigio, Wesley G. Skogan, and Robert C. Davis. Newbury Park, CA: Sage.

Gagne, Patricia. 1998. *Battered women's justice*. New York: Twayne.

Gelles, Richard J. 1974. *The violent home: A study of physical aggression between husbands and wives*. Newbury Park, CA: Sage.

———. 1983. An exchange/social control theory. In *The dark side of families: Current family violence research*, ed. David Finkelhor, Richard J. Gelles, Gerald T. Hotaling. Beverly Hills, CA: Sage.

———, and Murray Strauss. 1988. *Intimate violence*. New York: Simon and Schuster.

Genders, Elaine, and Elaine Player. 1987. Women in prison: The treatment, the control, and the experience. In *Gender, crime, and justice*, ed. Pat Carlen and Anne Worrall. Philadelphia: Open University Press.

Gibbs, Nancy. 1997. 'Til death do us part. In *Crisis in American institutions*, ed. Jerome H. Skolnick and Elliot Currie. New York: Longman.

Gillespie, Cynthia K. 1989. *Justifiable homicide*. Columbus: Ohio State University Press.

Gilliard, Darrell K., and Allen J. Beck. 1998. *Prisoners in 1997*. Washington, DC: U.S. Department of Justice.

Goetting, Ann. 1995. *Homicide in families and other special populations*. New York: Springer.

Goode, William. 1971. Force and violence in the family. *Journal of Marriage and the Family* 33:624–636.

Goolkasian, Gail A. 1986. "The judicial system and domestic violence—An expanding role." *Response* 9:2–7

Graham, Dee L. R., Edna Rawlings, and Nelly Rimini. 1990. Battered women, hostages, and the Stockholm syndrome. In *Feminist perspectives on wife abuse*, ed. Kersti Yllo and Michele Bograd. Newbury Park, CA: Sage.

Greenfeld, Lawrence A., Michael R. Rand, Diane Craven, Patsy A. Klaus, Craig A. Perkins, Cheryl Ringel, Greg Warchol, Cathy Maston, and James Alan Fox. 1998. *Violence by intimates*. Washington, DC: U.S. Department of Justice.

———, and Tracy L. Snell. 1999. *Women offenders*. Washington, DC: U.S. Department of Justice.

Hamby, Sherry L. 1998. Partner violence: Prevention and intervention. In *Partner violence*, ed. Jana L. Jasinski and Linda M. Williams. Thousand Oaks, CA: Sage.

Hargreaves, John. 2000. Battle over board of prison terms. *Verdict* 6:27–29. July.

Harlow, Caroline Wolf. 1999. *Prior abuse reported by inmates and probationers*. Washington, DC: U.S. Department of Justice.

Hart, Barbara J. 1990a. Assessing whether batterers will kill. Retrieved July 15, 1999 http://www.mincava.umn.edu/hart/lethali.htm.

————. 1990b. Domestic violence intervention system: A model for response to woman abuse. Retrieved July 15, 1999 http://www.mincava. umn.edu/hart/dvinter.htm.

————. 1992. Battered women and the criminal justice system. *American Behavioral Scientist* 36 (5): 624–638.

Hassine, Victor. 1996. *Life without parole: Living in prison today*. Los Angeles: Roxbury.

Healey, Kerry, Christine Smith, and Chris O'Sullivan. 1998. *Batterer intervention: Program approaches and criminal justice strategies*. Washington, DC: U.S. Department of Justice.

Heise, Lori L. 1994. *Violence against women: The hidden health burden*. Washington, DC: The World Bank.

————, Alanagh Raikes, Charlotte H. Watts, and Anthony B. Zwi. 1994. Violence against women: A neglected public health issue in less developed countries. *Social Science and Medicine* 39 (9): 1165–1179.

Hofford, Merridith, and Adele V. Harrell. 1993. *Family violence: Interventions for the justice system*. Washington, DC: Bureau of Justice Assistance.

Hondagneu-Sotelo, Pierette. 1996. Immigrant women and paid domestic work: Research, theory, and activism. In *Feminism and social change: Bridging theory and practice*, ed. Heidi Gottfried. Chicago: University of Illinois Press.

Human Rights Watch. 1996. *All too familiar: Sexual abuse of women in US state prisons*. New York: Human Rights Watch.

Hyden, Margareta. 1994. *Woman battering as marital act*. Oslo, Norway: Scandinavian University Press.

Jacobs, Michelle S. 1998. Requiring battered women die: Murder liability for mothers under failure to protect statutes. *Journal of Criminal Law and Criminology* 88 (2): 579–660.

James, William H., Carolyn West, and Karla Ezrre Deters. 2000. Youth dating violence. *Adolescence* 35 (139): 455–465.

Johann, Sara Lee, and Frank Osanka. 1989. Introduction. In *Representing . . . Battered women who kill*, ed. Sara Lee Johann and Frank Osanka. Springfield, IL: Charles C. Thomas.

Jolin, Annette, William Feyerherm, Robert Fountain, and Sharon Friedman. 1998. *Beyond arrest: the Portland, Oregon domestic violence experiment, final report*. Washington, DC: U.S. Department of Justice.

Jones, Ann. 1994. *Next time she'll be dead: Battering and how to stop it*. Boston: Beacon Press.

————. 1996. *Women who kill.* Boston: Beacon.

Jose, Maria Christina Y. 1985. *Women doing life sentences: A phenomenological study.* Ph.D. dissertation. Department of Education, University of Michigan.

Kandel, Minouche, and Kenneth J. Theisen. 1008. Revitalising the clemency movement. *San Francisco Daily Journal,* December 3.

Kantor, Glenda Kaufman, and Jana L. Jasinkski. 1998. Dynamics and risk factors in partner violence. In *Partner violence,* ed. Jana L. Jasinski and Linda M. Williams. Thousand Oaks, CA: Sage.

Karmen, Andrew. 1995. Women victims of crime. In *The criminal justice system and women,* ed. Barbara Raffel Price and Natalie J. Sokoloff. New York: McGraw-Hill.

Kelly, Liz. 1990. How women define their experiences of violence. In *Feminist perspectives on wife abuse,* ed. Kersti Yllo and Michele Bograd. Newbury Park, CA: Sage.

Kurz, Demie. 1993. Physical assaults by husbands: A major social problem. In *Current controversies on family violence,* ed. Richard J. Gelles and Donileen R. Loseke. Newbury Park, CA: Sage.

Langan, Patrick A., and John M. Dawson. 1995. *Spouse murder defendants in large urban counties.* Washington, DC: U.S. Department of Justice.

Langford, Linda, Nancy Isaac, and Stacey Kabat. 1998. Homicides related to intimate partner violence in Massachusetts. *Homicide Studies* 2 (4): 353–377.

Lattimore, Pamela K., James Trudeau, K. Jack Riley, Jordan Leiter, and Steven Edwards. 1997. *Homicide in eight US cities: Trends, contest, and policy implications.* Washington, DC: U.S. Department of Justice.

Laub, John H. 1990. Patterns of criminal victimization in the United States. In *Victims of crime: Problems, policies, and programs,* ed. Arthur J. Lurigio, Wesley G. Skogan, and Robert C. Davis. Newbury Park, CA: Sage.

Leonard, Elizabeth Dermody. 2000. Convicted survivors: A California study of women imprisoned for killing abusive spouses. *Women, Girls, & Criminal Justice* 1 (1): 5–6, 15.

Levinson, David. 1989. *Family violence in cross-cultural perspective.* Newbury Park, CA: Sage.

Liss, Marsha B., and Geraldine Butts Stahly. 1993. Domestic violence and child custody. In *Battering and family therapy,* ed. Marsali Hansen and Michele Harway. Newbury Park, CA: Sage.

Lott, Bernice. 1994. *Women's lives: Themes and variations in gender learning*. Pacific Grove, CA: Brooks/Cole.

Lott, Lonald D. 1995. Deadly secrets: Violence in the police family. *FBI Law Enforcement Bulletin* 64 (11): 12–16.

Lundgren, Eva. 1995. *Feminist theory and violent empiricism*. Aldershot, UK: Avebury.

Maguigan, Holly. 1991. Battered women and self-defense: Myths and misconceptions in current reform proposals. *University of Pennsylvania Law Review* 140:379–486.

Maguire, Kathleen, and A. L. Pastore, eds. 1996. *Sourcebook of criminal justice statistics 1995*. Washington, DC: Government Printing Office.

Mahoney, Martha A. 1991. Legal images of battered women: Redefining the issue of separation. *Michigan Law Review* 90:1–94.

Mahoney, Patricia, and Linda M. Williams. 1998. Sexual assault in marriage. In *Partner violence*, ed. Jana L. Jasinski and Linda M. Williams. Thousand Oaks, CA: Sage.

Makepeace, James M. 1999. Courtship violence among college students. In *Family violence: Studies from the social sciences and professions Vol. 2 relationship violence* 2nd ed., ed. James M. Makepeace. New York: McGraw-Hill.

Mann, Coramae Richey. 1989. Getting even? Women who kill in domestic encounters. In *Representing . . . Battered women who kill*, ed. Sara Lee Johann and Frank Osanka. Springfield, IL: Charles C. Thomas.

———. 1992. Female murderers and their motives: A tale of two cities. In *Representing . . . Battered women who kill*, ed. Sara Lee Johann and Frank Osanka. Springfield, IL: Charles C. Thomas.

Marcus, Isabel. 1994. Reframing "domestic violence": Terrorism in the home. In *The public nature of private violence: The discovery of domestic abuse*, ed. Martha Albertson Fineman and Roxanne Mykitiuk. New York: Routledge.

Marcus, Maria L. 1981. Conjugal violence: The law of force and the force of law. *California Law Review* 69:1657–1733.

Martin, Del. 1983. *Battered wives*. New York: Pocket Books.

Martin, Sandra L., Linda Mackie, Lawrence L. Kupper, Paul A. Buescher, and Kathryn E. Moracco. 2001. Physical abuse of women before, during, and after pregnancy. *Journal of the American Medical Association* 285 (12): 1581–1584.

Marvin, Douglas R. 1997. The dynamics of domestic abuse. *Annual editions: Criminal justice 98/99*. Guilford, CT: Dushkin.

McCorkel, Jill A. 1996. Justice, gender, and incarceration: An analysis of the leniency and severity debate. In *Examining the justice process*, ed. James A. Inciardi. Fort Worth, TX: Harcourt Brace.

McFarlane, Judith, Barbara Parker, Karen Soeken, and Linda Bullock. 1992. *Journal of the American Medical Association* 267: 3176–3178.

McHardy, Louis H. and Meredith Hofford. 1998. *Family violence: Emerging programs for battered mothers and their children.* Reno: National Council of Juvenile and Family Court Judges.

McLeer, Susan V., and Rebecca Anwar. 1989. A study of battered women presenting in an emergency department. *American Journal of Public Health* 79:65–66.

Mercy, James A., and Linda E. Saltzman. 1989. Fatal violence among spouses in the United States, 1976–85. *American Journal of Public Health* 79:595–599.

Miller, Susan L. 1993. Arrest policies for domestic violence and their implications for battered women. In *It's a crime: Women and justice*, ed. Roslyn Muraskin and Ted Alleman. Englewood Cliffs, NJ: Prentice-Hall.

Molidor, Christian, and Richard M. Tolman. 1998. Gender and contextual factors in adolescent dating violence. *Violence Against Women* 4 (2): 180–194.

Moracco, Kathryn E., Carol W. Runyan, and John D. Butts. 1998. Femicide in North Carolina, 1991–1993. *Homicide Studies* 2 (4): 422–446.

Morash, Merry, Timothy S. Bynum, and Barbara A. Koons. 1998. *Women offenders: Programming needs and promising approaches.* Washington, DC: U.S. Department of Justice.

Murphy, Christopher M., and K. Daniel O'Leary. 1994. Research paradigms, values, and spouse abuse. *Journal of Interpersonal Violence* 9:207–223.

Murzak, Peter M., Kenneth Tardiff, and Charles S. Hirsch. 1992. The epidemiology of murder-suicide. *Journal of the American Medical Association* 267:3179–3183.

National Clearinghouse for the Defense of Battered Women. 1994. *Statistics Packet: 3rd Edition.* Philadelphia: National Clearinghouse for the Defense of Battered Women.

Neuman, W. Lawrence. 1994. *Social research methods.* Boston: Allyn and Bacon.

O'Dell, Anne. 1996. Domestic violence homicides. *The Police Chief* 63 (2): 21–23.

O'Shea, Kathleen. 1993, Women on death row. In *Women prisoners: A forgotten population*, ed. Beverly R. Fletcher, Lynda Dixon Shaver, and Dreama Moon. Westport, CT: Praeger.

Osthoff, Sue. 1991. Restoring justice: Clemency for battered women. *Response* 14:2–3.

———. 2001. When victims become defendants: Battered women charged with crimes. In *Women, crime, and criminal justice*, ed. Claire M. Renzetti and Lynne Goodstein. Los Angeles: Roxbury.

Owen, Barbara, and Barbara Bloom. 1995. Profiling women prisoners: Findings from national surveys and a California sample. *The Prison Journal* 75 (2): 165–185.

Pagelow, Mildred Daley. 1981. *Woman battering*. Beverly Hills, CA: Sage.

———. 1984. *Family violence*. New York: Praeger.

———. 1985. The "battered husband syndrome": Social problem or much ado about little? In *Marital violence*, ed. Norman Johnson. London: Routledge.

———. 1992. Adult victims of domestic violence. *Journal of Interpersonal Violence* 7:87–120.

Parrish, Janet. 1996. Trend analysis: Expert testimony on battering and its effects in criminal cases. *Wisconsin Women's Law Journal* 11 (1): 75–173.

Payne, Lee. 1996. Training is key. *The Police Chief* 63 (2): 55–58.

Pincus, Gail. 1997. Author's personal communication with Gail Pincus, Director of Domestic Abuse Center, Northridge, CA.

Pleck, Elizabeth. 1987. *Domestic tyranny*. New York: Oxford University Press.

Ptacek, James. 1990. Why do men batter their wives? In *Feminist perspectives on wife abuse*, ed. Kersti Yllo and Michele Bograd. Newbury Park, CA: Sage.

———. 1997. The tactics and strategies of men who batter. In *Violence between intimate partners*, ed. Albert P. Cardarelli. Boston: Allyn and Bacon.

Randall, T. 1991. Duluth takes firm stance against domestic violence; mandates abuser arrest, education. *Journal of the American Medical Association*: 1184.

Rapaport, Elizabeth. 1994. The death penalty and the domestic discount. In *The public nature of private violence*, ed. Martha Albertson Fineman and Roxanne Mykitiuk. New York: Routledge.

Rasche, Christine E. 1990. Early models for contemporary thought in domestic violence and women who kill their mates: A review of the literature from 1895 to 1970. *Women & Criminal Justice* 1:31–53.

———. 1995. Minority women and domestic violence: The unique dilemmas of battered women of color. In *The criminal justice system and women*, ed. Barbara Raffel Price and Natalie J. Sokoloff. New York: McGraw Hill.

Rennison, Callie Marie, and Sarah Welchans. 2000. *Intimate partner violence*. Washington, DC: U.S. Department of Justice.

Renzetti, Claire M., and Raymond M. Lee. 1993. The use of feminist methodologies researching sensitive topics. In *Researching sensitive topics*, ed. Claire M. Renzetti and Raymond M. Lee. Newbury Park, CA: Sage.

Roth, Rachel. 2000. Adding insult to injury: New York charges battered mothers with neglect. Available online. http://www.salon.com/mwt/feature/2000/09/14/battered_mothers/index.html.

Saunders, Daniel G. 1995. The tendency to arrest victims of domestic violence. *Journal of Interpersonal Violence* 10:147–158.

Schafran, Lynn Hecht. 1990. Overwhelming evidence: Reports on gender bias in the courts. *Trial* 26:28–35.

———. 1991. Update: Gender bias in the courts. *Trial* 27:112–118.

Schmidt, Janell D., and Lawrence W. Sherman. 1996. Does arrest deter domestic violence? In *Do arrests and restraining orders work?* ed. Eve S. Buzawa and Carl G. Buzawa. Thousand Oaks, CA: Sage

Schneider, Elizabeth M. 1986. Describing and changing: Women's self-defense work and the problem of expert testimony on battering. *Women's Rights Law Reporter* 9:195–225.

———. 1992. Particularity and generality: Challenges of feminist theory and practice in work on woman-abuse. *New York University Law Review* 67:520–568.

———. 2000. *Battered women and feminist lawmaking*. New Haven, CT: Yale University Press.

———, Susan B. Jordan, and Cristina C. Arguedas. 1981. In *Women's self-defense cases*, ed. Elizabeth Bochnak. Charlottesville, VA: The Michie Company.

Schuler, Margaret A. 1996. Introduction. In *State responses to domestic violence: Current status and needed improvements*, ed. Rebecca P. Sewall, Arati Vasan, and Margaret A. Schuler. Washington, DC: Women, Law & Development International.

Sedlak, Andrea J. 1988. Prevention of wife abuse. In *Handbook of family violence*, ed. Vincent B. Van Hasselt, Randall L. Morrison, Alan S. Bellack, and Michel Hersen. New York: Plenum Press.

Sengupta, Somini. 2000. Tough justice: Taking a child when one parent is battered. *New York Times*, July 8. Available online. http://www.sanctuaryforfamilies.org/index16a.htm.

Shaw, Nancy Stoller. 1982. Female patients and the medical profession in jails and prisons. In *Judge, lawyer, victim, thief*, ed. Nicole Hahn Rafter and Elizabeth Anne Stanko. Boston: Northeastern University Press.

Sherman, Lawrence. 1988. *Domestic violence*. Washington, DC: U.S. Department of Justice.

———. 1992. *Policing domestic violence*. New York: Free Press.

Siegel, Larry J. 1998. *Criminology*. Belmont, CA: Wadsworth.

Silverman, Jay G., Anita Raj, Lorelei A. Mucci, and Jeanne E. Hathaway. 2001. Dating violence against adolescent girls and associated substance use, unhealthy weight control, sexual risk behavior, pregnancy, and suicidality. *Journal of the American Medical Association* 286: 572–579.

Sipe, Beth, and Evelyn J. Hall. 1996. *I am not your victim*. Thousand Oaks, CA: Sage.

Slambrouck, Paul Van. 2000. In more states, parole is a thing of the past. *Christian Science Monitor*, May 22, 2000.

Smith, Dorothy E. 1992. Sociology from women's experience: A reaffirmation. *Sociological Theory* 10:88–98.

Snell, Tracy L. 1994. *Women in prison*. Washington, DC: U.S. Department of Justice.

———. 1996. *Capital punishment 1995*. Washington, DC: U.S. Department of Justice.

Stark, Evan. 1990. Rethinking homicide: Violence, race, and the politics of gender. *International Journal of Health Services* 20:3–26.

———. 1996. Mandatory arrest of batterers: A reply to its critics. In *Do arrests and restraining orders work?* ed. Eve S. Buzawa and Carl G. Buzawa. Thousand Oaks, CA: Sage.

———, and Anne H. Flitcraft. 1988. Violence among intimates: An epidemiological review. In *Handbook on family violence*, ed. Vincent B. Van Hasselt, Randall L. Morrison, Alan S. Bellack, and Michel Hersen. New York: Plenum.

———. 1996. *Women at risk: Domestic violence and women's health*. Thousand Oaks, CA: Sage.

Steffensmeier, Darrell, and Emilie Allan. 1996. Gender and crime: Toward a gendered theory of female offending. *Annual Review of Sociology* 22:459–487.

Stinchcombe, Jeanne B., and Vernon B. Fox. 1999. *Introduction to corrections 5/e.* Upper Saddle River, NJ: Prentice-Hall.

Stout, Karen D. 1991. Women who kill: Offenders or defenders. *Affilia* 6:8–22.

———, and Patricia Brown. 1995. Legal and social differences between men and women who kill intimate partners. *Affilia* 10:194–205.

Straus, Murray A. 1980. Wife-beating: How common and why. In *The social causes of husband-wife violence*, ed. Murray A. Straus and Gerald T. Hotaling. Minneapolis: University of Minnesota.

———. 1993. Physical assaults by wives: A major social problem. In *Current controversies on family violence*, ed. Richard J. Gelles and Donileen R. Loseke. Newbury, CA: Sage.

———, Richard Gelles, and Suzanne Steinmetz. 1980. *Behind closed doors.* Garden City, NY: Doubleday.

Streib, Victor L. 1992. Death penalty for battered women. *Florida State University Law Review* 20:163–194.

———. 2001. Death penalty for female offenders. Retrieved March 2001. http://www.law.onu.edu/faculty/streib/femdeath.htm.

Sugg, Nancy K., Robert S. Thompson, Diane C. Thompson, Roland Maiuro, and Frederick P. Rivara. 1999. Domestic violence and primary care. *Archives of Family Medicine* 8:301–306.

Sullivan Cris M. 1997. Societal collusion and culpability in intimate male violence. In *Violence between intimate partners*, ed. Albert P. Cardarelli. Boston: Allyn and Bacon.

The Sentencing Project. 2001. *U.S. surpasses Russia as world leader in rate of incarceration.* Washington, DC: The Sentencing Project.

———. 1999. *Facts about prisons and prisoners.* Retrieved November 1999. http://www.sentencing project.org/brief/1035.htm. 8/99.

———. 1997. *Americans behind bars: US and international use of incarceration 1995.* Retrieved November 1999. http://sproject.com/test/pubs/tsppubs/9030data.html.

Tjaden, Patricia, and Nancy Thoennes. 1998. *Prevalence, incidence, and consequences of violence against women: Findings from the national violence against women survey.* Washington, DC: U.S. Department of Justice.

———. 2000. *Extent, nature, and consequences of intimate partner violence.* Washington, DC: U.S. Department of Justice.

Totman, Jane. 1978. *The murderess: A psychosocial study of criminal homicide.* San Francisco: R & E Research Associates.

UNICEF. 2000. Domestic violence against women and girls. *Innocenti Digest* No. 6, May. Florence, Italy.

U.S. Commission on Civil Rights. 1982. *Under the rule of thumb: Battered women and the administration of justice.* Washington, DC: U.S. Government Printing Office.

U.S. Congress Senate Special Committee on Aging. 1991. *Reducing the use of chemical restraints in nursing homes.* Washington, DC: U.S. Government Printing Office.

U.S. Conference of Mayors. 1998. *A status report on hunger and homelessness in America's cities: 1998.* Washington, DC: U.S. Conference of Mayors.

Violence Against Women Grants Office [VAWGO]. 1997. *Domestic violence and stalking: The second annual report to Congress under the Violence Against Women Act.* Washington, DC: U.S. Department of Justice.

Walker, Lenore E. 1979. *The battered woman.* New York: Harper and Row.

———. 1987. When the battered woman becomes the defendant. In *Crime and its victims: International research and public policy issues,* ed. Emilio C. Viano. New York: Hemisphere.

———. 1989. *Terrifying love: Why battered women kill and how society responds.* New York: Harper and Row.

———. 1992. Battered women syndrome and self-defense. *Notre Dame Journal of Law, Ethics & Public Policy* 6:321–334.

Welling, Bobbie L., Andrea Biren, Marian Johnston, Sheila Kuehl, and Diane Nunn. 1990. *Achieving equal justice for women and men in the courts: The draft report of the Judicial Council Advisory Committee on Gender Bias in the Courts.* San Francisco: Judicial Council of California.

Wiehe, Vernon R., and Ann L. Richards. 1995. *Intimate betrayal.* Thousand Oaks, CA: Sage.

Wilson, K. J. 1997. *When violence begins at home.* Alameda, CA: Hunter House.

Wilson, Margo, and Martin Daly. 1993. Spousal homicide risk and estrangement. *Violence and Victims* 8 (1): 3–16.

———, Holly Johnson, and Martin Daly. 1995. Lethal and nonlethal violence against wives. *Canadian Journal of Criminology* 37:331–361.

Wilson, Nanci Koser. 1993. Gendered interaction in criminal homicide. In *Homicide: The victim-offender connection*, ed. Anna Victoria Wilson. Cincinnati: Anderson.

Wolak, Janis, and David Finkelhor. 1998. Children exposed to partner violence. In *Partner violence*, ed. Jana L. Jasinski and Linda M. Williams. Thousand Oaks, CA: Sage.

Wolfgang, Marvin E. 1967. A sociological analysis of criminal homicide. In *Studies in homicide*, ed. Marvin E. Wolfgang. New York: Harper and Row.

Yllo, Kersti, and Michele Bograd, eds. 1988. *Feminist perspectives on wife abuse*. Newbury Park: Sage.

Zawitz, Marianne W. 1994. *Violence between intimates*. Washington, DC: U.S. Department of Justice.

Zorza, Joan. 1997. Battered women behave like other threatened victims. *Focus: Los Angeles County Domestic Violence Council News Quarterly* 3 (2): 7.

Author Index

Subject Index